LOCATION AND TRADE THEORY

Industrial Location, Comparative Advantage,
and the Geographic Pattern of Production
in the United States

by

Joseph Thomas Johnson
United States Air Force

THE UNIVERSITY OF CHICAGO
DEPARTMENT OF GEOGRAPHY
RESEARCH PAPER NO. 198

1981

Library of Congress Cataloging in Publication Data

Johnson, Joseph Thomas, 1946–
    Location and trade theory.
    (Research paper / University of Chicago, Dept. of Geography; no. 198)
    Bibliography: p. 107

    1. Industries, Location of. 2. Commerce. 3. Comparative advantage (Commerce) 4. Industries, Location of—United States. I. Title. II. Series: Research paper (University of Chicago. Dept. of Geography; no. 198)

H31.C514 no. 198 [HC79.D5] 910s [338.6'042] 81-11558
ISBN 0-89065-105-1 (pbk.)   AACR2

Research Papers are available from:

The University of Chicago
Department of Geography
5828 S. University Avenue
Chicago, Illinois 60637
Price: $8.00; $6.00 series subscription.

To Deborah, who paid for it.

TABLE OF CONTENTS

v

LIST OF TABLES

LIST OF FIGURES

ACKNOWLEDGMENTS

I owe many thanks to my advisor, Professor Donald W. Jones, for teaching me to treat economic geography as the economic analysis of geographic systems. His observations contributed to both the manuscript and the knowledge on which it is based.

I wish to thank Professor Chauncy D. Harris for making a number of helpful comments on the manuscript. I wish also to thank Professor Michael P. Conzen for reading the manuscript.

Finally, I wish to express my appreciation to the Department of Geography of the University of Chicago for providing me with a superb environment in which to earn my doctorate.

CHAPTER I

INTRODUCTION AND OUTLINE

OF THE MONOGRAPH

This monograph is an essay about location theory and the study of industrial location patterns. It proceeds from the general to the specific in its consideration of theories and techniques of industrial location analysis. First, a general industrial location model is developed. This is followed by a discussion of an important special case of the general model. Finally, the use of the model in economic geographic research is illustrated by the presentation of empirical tests of the special case.

Chapter II of this monograph is a discussion of industrial location theories that assume either fixed regional resources or fixed final goods prices. It is pointed out that the assumption of fixed resources renders a model most applicable to short-run situations in which resource supply reactions are minimal. The assumption of fixed prices holds demand constant and thereby renders a theory an analysis of production location rather than market location.

Two of the most important arguments in chapter II pertain to the neglected role of site rent in neoclassical location theory and the correspondence between location theory and trade theory. With regard to site rent, it is argued that the plant location model of Alfred Weber[1] is incomplete without a provision for the rent that arises from transport costs, as analyzed by Thünen.[2] With regard to trade theory, it is argued that the logic of Weber's idea of locational pull is basically the same as the logic of comparative advantage used by trade theorists such as Ricardo and Ohlin.[3] Weber

---

[1] Alfred Weber, Theory of the Location of Industries, trans. Carl J. Friedrich (Chicago: University of Chicago Press, 1929).

[2] Johann H. von Thünen, Von Thünen's Isolated State, trans. Carla M. Wartenburg and ed. Peter Hall (Oxford: Pergamon Press, 1966). Originally published as Der isolierte Staat in Beziehung auf Landwirtschaft und Nationalökonomie (Hamburg, 1826).

[3] David Ricardo, The Principles of Political Economy and Taxation (London: J. Murray, 1821); Bertil Ohlin, Interregional and International Trade, rev. ed. (Cambridge: Harvard University Press, 1967).

predicts <u>which location</u> will produce <u>given goods</u> while Ohlin predicts <u>which goods</u> will be produced by <u>given locations;</u> but both theorists predict on the basis of comparative costs among locations.

Chapter III is a formalization of the more literary discussion in chapter II of location under conditions of fixed regional resources and final good prices. A nonlinear programming version of the Weber location model that includes the rent analysis of transport by Thünen is demonstrated to be the programming dual of a nonlinear programming version of elements of Ohlin's trade theory. The existence of such duality means that when there is a solution to the Ohlin output proportions problem, there is also a solution to the Weber least-cost location problem for the same fixed resources and prices. It is argued that this duality permits those location problems involving fixed regional resources and prices to be analyzed with trade theory. The assumption of finite and immobile regional resources provides a clear basis for distinguishing one producing region from another according to production possibilities, while holding demand facing a region constant in the form of fixed prices allows trade theory to work as a theory of production location without requiring it to explain why a region exports a certain proportion of its output instead of consuming it.

Chapter IV of this monograph develops a particular case of the general location model developed in chapter II. Whereas the general model treats both intraregional and interregional aspects of industrial location, the particular case is concerned only with the interregional aspects of location under conditions of finite resources and constant demand. This special case stresses the trade-theoretic portions of the general model. That is, intraregional transport costs are assumed to be zero, so no site rent accrues because of distance. Each region is, in effect, collapsed into a point and the stress of the analysis is on production differences among these points that arise from their geographic characteristics, especially their received output prices and the proportions in which they possess various resources.

This chapter demonstrates that the additional assumption of constant cost production technology renders the interregional case of the general model identical to the general equilibrium model developed by Jones.[1] That is, the intertemporal implications of Jones's model can also be interpreted as interregional implications.

---

[1] Ronald W. Jones, "The Structure of Simple General Equilibrium Models," <u>Journal of Political Economy</u> 73 (December 1965): 557-72.

Hence, two powerful hypotheses can be derived for location theory just as for trade theory. They predict, respectively, a correlation of interregional differences in factor endowments with output proportions and a correlation of interregional differences in received output prices with relative factor wages.

Chapter V addresses the problem of generalizing Jones's hypotheses, which are proven only for the case of two goods and two factors.[1] It is argued that the basic tendencies embodied in the two-by-two results persist in certain cases where a region produces multiple goods with multiple factors. The real problem is how to determine which factor endowment proportions affect which output proportions and which received price ratios affect which wage ratios. By using Kemp's principle for associating goods and factors on the basis of high production coefficient ratios,[2] it is argued that the powerful interregional hypotheses in chapter IV can be generated for the multi-good, multi-factor case. That is, the two-by-two results can be shown to apply to certain goods that are selected with a knowledge of their relative factor intensities.

Chapter VI of this monograph recapitulates the terms and assumptions of the model developed in the four prior chapters in order to evaluate the possible uses of the model in economic geographic research. It is a sort of bridge between the theoretical chapters and the final empirical chapter. It is suggested that the model can be most appropriately applied to those space-economies that are amenable to general equilibrium and cross-sectional analysis. However, the complexity and integration that usually characterize such economies can pose difficulties for empirical testing of the resource-output and price-wage hypotheses generated by the interregional special case of the model. Ways to reduce these difficulties are suggested by way of introducing the next (and empirical) chapter.

Chapter VII is intended to be more illustrative than definitive in its empirical analysis. That is, empirical tests are constructed and performed in order to illustrate that the theoretical chapters of the monograph can be made to yield concrete hypotheses about the real world. The resource-output result of the model developed in chapters IV and V is tested with United States

---

[1]Ibid.

[2]Murray C. Kemp, The Pure Theory of International Trade and Investment (Englewood Cliffs, N.J.: Prentice-Hall, 1969), chap. 1, Appendix.

regional natural resource and manufacturing data. This amounts to a regional test of the well-known Heckscher-Ohlin trade theory of factor proportions, which has been tested before. The present analysis, however, is one of the very few (perhaps the only) to compare factor endowment ratios with output ratios.

Chapter VIII contains a brief summary of the entire monograph.

CHAPTER II

TRADE THEORY AS LOCATION THEORY

This chapter explores the proposition that patterns of industrial location can be studied with trade theory. In general, countries trade what they produce; so a theory of trade is, at least implicitly, a theory of the location of production. As Bertil Ohlin observes,

> trade theory verges on location theory. Instead of asking why certain countries exchange certain goods with one another, one can ask why production is divided between these countries in a certain way.[1]

This chapter does not advocate applying the whole of trade theory to industrial location. Rather, it suggests distinguishing, whenever possible, aspects of trade theory that pertain specifically to production from aspects that pertain specifically to the interregional exchange of commodities. Although exchange is essential to general equilibrium and therefore affects industrial geography, it is also true that many useful hypotheses about production location can be generated from trade theory without incurring the burden of explaining why a certain proportion of a region's output is consumed at home rather than exported.

In particular, trade theories of regional comparative advantage in input costs can be shown to rest on logic that closely resembles the basis for theories of Alfred Weber and others about the locational pull of productive factors. This connection between trade and location affords the location theorist powerful tools of analysis in addition to the traditional approaches of location theory, especially if production output data rather than trade flow data are analyzed by trade theory.

Before discussing the correspondence between trade and location, however, it is necessary to review the basic insights of Weber's treatise and to take account of Moses's extension of it for the case of variable factor proportions in production.[2] In addition, this essay will argue that Weber's analysis of

---

[1] Ohlin, Trade, p. 307.

[2] Weber, Location of Industries; Leon Moses, "Location and the Theory of Production," Quarterly Journal of Economics 72 (1958): 259-72.

locational cost savings is incomplete without a provision for Thünen's
derivation of site rent from differential location costs.[1]

Weber's Theory of Industrial Location and the Theory of Site Rent

Weber looks at industrial location from the standpoint of a
plant's desire to minimize production and transport costs with
respect to a given market offering a given price for the produced
commodity. He takes the locations of labor and raw materials as
given. At each labor location, supply is assumed to be perfectly
elastic (i.e., inexhaustible) at a wage constant over all occupa-
tions.[2] Raw materials are priced according to the cost of transporting them from their original sites to the location of production,
with the "transport cost" being weighted to account for different
F.O.B. prices of the same material at different sites.[3] Since not
all resources (i.e., labor and raw materials) necessary to produce
output for a "given amount of consumption" can be found at any one
place, it advantages the plant to locate where the sum of transport
(including raw materials) costs and labor costs is at a minimum.[4]

Costs of transporting the output to market also contribute to
the cost at a production site; but, since both the market location
and price are assumed given, distribution costs can be accounted
part of the total cost of producing the delivered good. Then the
overall problem addressed by the Weber model is total cost minimization with respect to a given level of output.

Weber's theory requires some modification because it is inadequate in its treatment of two important locational influences:
site rent and variable factor proportions in production. A neglect
of site rent is revealed when Weber argues that, if two sites are
equidistant from the market, a site that affords lower transport
costs of raw materials will be less desirable than a site that
contains labor so cheap that savings in labor costs can more than
offset the increased transport costs of moving away from the cheap
raw materials location.[5] What Weber fails to discuss is the possibility that some, or even all, of the savings accruing to the
producer because of location will be extracted as location rent in
a manner first analyzed by Thünen.[6]

---

[1] Thünen, Isolated State.

[2] Weber, Location of Industries, p. 38.

[3] Ibid., p. 34.   [4] Ibid., pp. 48ff. and 102ff.   [5] Ibid., pp. 102-03.

[6] Thünen, Isolated State, part 1, chaps. 4, 5A, 5B; part 2, sect. 2, frag. 2.

In competitive markets,[1] rival producers will use the potential
surplus of revenues over operating costs afforded by a site to bid
for use of the site, thereby driving up the rent, perhaps to the
limit of the "savings," which also will be the value of the land to
the producer.[2] Although this means producers within the same industry could be found locating indifferently at a variety of sites
within an area yielding "surplus,"[3] location need not be indeterminate between industries, because different industries have different "surplus" areas due to different operating cost functions
and different demand schedules. Therefore, some industries can
afford to bid higher than others for sites in the same area.[4]

Weber does discuss site rent when he analyzes the effect on
location of what he calls "agglomerative" forces: external economies
that result from the concentration of industry in a given area. In
particular, he names the availability of more industrial services,
a better organized and trained labor pool, and better municipal
services. He then posits a counteracting effect on agglomeration of
rising land values as more plants locate in the same area;[5] but he
does not make a direct connection between agglomeration economies
and site rent. Jones clarifies the direct relationship between
urban externalities and urban land values: depending on the number
of plants bidding for sites within the industrial agglomeration and
depending on the relative bargaining acumens of landlord and producer, some or all of the "savings" that accrue to a plant from
locating where it can benefit from external economies will be extracted as site rent.[6]

---

[1]Weber, _Location of Industries_, discusses both price competition (pp. 18-19)
and monopoly pricing in regard to intra-industry market structure. In regard to
inter-industry competition for location, his discussion of agglomeration economies
(chap. 5) implies an assumption that many producers, from any number of industries,
can bid for use of the same site.

[2]Benjamin H. Stevens, "Linear Programming and Location Rent," _Journal of
Regional Science_ 3 (1963): 15-26.

[3]Walter Isard, _Location and Space-Economy_ (Cambridge: MIT Press, 1956),
pp. 196-97, 202.

[4]Edgar M. Hoover, _The Location of Economic Activity_ (New York: McGraw-Hill,
1948), pp. 94-96; William Alonso, _Location and Land Use_ (Cambridge: Harvard
University Press, 1964), chap. 5.

[5]Weber, _Location of Industries_, pp. 129-31.

[6]Donald W. Jones, "Location and the Demand for Non-Traded Goods: A
Generalization of the Theory of Site Rent," _Journal of Regional Science_, 20
(1980): 331-42.

Basically, then, the availability of agglomeration economies and the availability of labor or raw materials are functionally similar circumstances. In either case, Weber's theory has the resources of an area--labor, raw materials, or services--exerting pulls on industry that are functions of their roles in production and their costs relative to the costs in other areas. Site rent, however, can counteract the pulls.

Besides a revising for rent, Weber's theory needs a revising in the matter of input coefficients. Weber makes his model unnecessarily inflexible by assuming that a plant produces a given level of output with fixed proportions of inputs.[1] Moses offers a rigorous model of location based on the economic theory of the optimizing firm, including factor substitution. For a given demand, such as assumed by Weber, firms can choose their input proportions and their locations simultaneously; so inputs are substituted one for another until their ratios of marginal productivity to marginal delivered cost are all equal and therefore cost is minimized.[2]

Although the additions of Thünen's rent analysis and Moses's variable proportions analysis do modify Weber's model, they do not change it in any basic way. The modified version still retains the essential Weberian insight into the pull of a location's resources on industry.

Location and the Theory of Comparative Advantage

Weber's concept of locational pull provides a basis for a theory of regional comparative advantage. Indeed, since the amount of pull a region exerts on an industry depends on production costs within the region compared to costs elsewhere, the Weber model can partially predict a region's comparative advantage. The model cannot totally predict comparative advantage because it has an incomplete concept of regional resources: these are assumed to be virtually infinite. Although Weber alludes to the eventual exhaustibility of an area's raw materials, in his formal model he has the plant or industry facing a perfectly elastic supply of labor and raw materials from any given resource site.[3] With unlimited resources, a regional economy lacks realistically finite production

---

[1] Weber, Location of Industries, pp. 111 and 227.

[2] Moses, "Location and Production."

[3] Weber, Location of Industries, pp. 73-74. Moses, "Location and Production," likewise takes the delivered prices of inputs as fixed and does not directly consider the possibility of inelastic supply at a given site.

possibilities: for demand perfectly elastic at a given price, the region is not constrained to pick and choose among possible combinations of goods to produce by allocating scarce resources to certain industries in certain proportions. Thus the Weber model can predict how much pull a region has for any industry; but, since the region is theoretically capable of producing as much as it wants of any good, the model cannot predict the region's pull on one industry relative to its pull on another industry.

Trade theories of comparative advantage, on the other hand, aim specifically at the explanation of a region's choice of which goods to produce in which proportions. Consequently, these theories contain assumptions about the limitations of regions' resource supplies which imply finite production possibilities: regions must allocate their limited resources among certain industries in certain proportions. Ricardo deduces that Portugal will specialize in the production of wine and import all its cloth from England because Portugal has a comparative advantage in wine: wine is relatively cheaper to produce--i.e., uses a lower proportion of the limited resources--in Portugal than in England. Even though it could produce both goods at an absolute cost of fewer resources than England, Portugal will acquire more cloth by leaving all its finite resource supply in wine production and using the surplus product to buy cloth from England (which has a comparative advantage in that good).[1] Whereas the Weber model (correctly) reveals Portugal to exert a pull on both the wine and cloth industries because of lower absolute production costs, the Ricardo model provides a rationale for choosing between those industries because of finite resources.

Ricardo effectively defines the boundaries of countries' space-economies when he assumes that countries' resources are entirely separate and unshared: resources are considered immobile between (but mobile within) countries. Though this simplifying assumption may at times be difficult to support with either intra-national or international data,[2] it does permit conceiving of

---

[1]Ricardo, Political Economy, chap. 7.

[2]Paul J. Schwind, Migration and Regional Development in the United States, Research Papers, no. 133 (Chicago: University of Chicago Department of Geography, 1971); Donald B. Freeman, International Trade Migration and Capital Flows, Research Papers, no. 146 (Chicago: University of Chicago Department of Geography, 1973).

regional production possibilities with a theoretical and empirical clarity that is hard to attain in the Weber model.[1]

With perfectly elastic demand, the only geographical limit on production in the Weber model is the total delivered cost of inputs: the model assumes that a firm or industry will not incur negative income by importing inputs from so far away that transport costs cause marginal cost to exceed marginal revenue. Yet this cost limitation is not sufficient to define a region's production possibilities completely when resources are assumed finite, because the potential resource supply areas of different production locations may overlap. Production possibilities can then only be completely defined when it is determined how regions compete with each other for use of the same limited resources. However, with free trade in final goods among regions already assumed, the addition of interregional resource competition leaves a trade or location model with very few features by which to define an economic region. It can be argued that complete mobility of factors and goods makes a purportedl interregional system into a single intraregional economy.[2]

While the Ricardian model is capable of defining regions and predicting their production specializations, it is, nevertheless, only of limited use in explaining the overall geographical pattern of production. This is because analysis in terms of a single composite production cost deprives the specification of a location's costs of geographic detail. The _individual_ costs making up total cost at a location reflect the local conditions that help determine the location's comparative advantage. However useful the composite cost approach may be for explaining trade flows, it obscures the productive uniqueness of a place: the elements which make one place distinguishable from others as an industrial location.

Rawstron outlines a theory of industrial location that is based on geographic variation. The key point is geographical limitation: at a given location, only certain kinds of production can profitably take place according to various local input cost and

[1] David L. Emerson, _Production, Location and the Automotive Agreement_ (Ottowa: Economic Council of Canada, 1975), does assume interregional resource immobility in his Weber-Moses approach to location costs.

[2] Louis Lefeber, _Allocation in Space_ (Amsterdam: North-Holland Publishing Co., 1958), presents a mathematical programming formulation of industrial location that allocates a region's resources to whatever region is optimal. See also J. Serck-Hanssen, _Optimal Patterns of Location_ (Amsterdam: North-Holland Publishing Co., 1971). Weber (_Location of Industries_, p. 38), in holding labor (but not raw materials) immobile does not limit production possibilities because, at the same time, he is taking the supply of labor at any location to be inexhaustible.

marketing cost conditions. Different kinds of production will require differing proportions of inputs and differing means of access
to different markets. The profitability of a location for a given
kind of production will depend on the relations among the components
of the production cost structure. To the degree that these cost
components vary spatially, production must vary spatially.[1]

Unlike the Ricardian theory of aggregated costs, Rawstron's
attention to the components of total production cost permits seeking
the causes of comparative advantage in the relations among these components. This, of course, is reminiscent of the Weber model's break-
down of locational pull according to types of costs ("transport-" or
"labor-orientation"). Thus, while the Ricardian model provides a concept of finite regional production possibilities, the Weber model provides a concept of geographically determined production capabilities.

The Heckscher-Ohlin Theory of
Factor Endowments

Though Weber bases his location theory on spatial variations
in resource costs, he does not undertake to explain why such variations occur. Heckscher and Ohlin offer a more complete version of
this theory, a general equilibrium explanation which recognizes that
costs are a result of industrial location as well as a cause of it.[2]
While acknowledging the implication of the Weber model that a region
produces commodities requiring relatively large proportions of
factors that are relatively cheap in the region, Heckscher and Ohlin
take the explanation further by reasoning that the cheaper factors
will tend to be the relatively abundant factors in the region.[3]
Thus the geographic pattern of comparative advantage derives in
large part from differences among regions in their proportional endowments of resources, which Ohlin, like Ricardo, considers finite,
mobile within regions, but immobile between regions.[4]

Furthermore, the very costs that attract industry to a region,
i.e., the low costs of abundant resources, will tend to rise as more
and more plants bid for the resources. At the same time, the region
will tend to import more of those goods that contain a high proportion of the region's relatively scarce resources. This will, in

---

[1] E. M. Rawstron, "Three Principles of Industrial Location," *Transactions,
Institute of British Geographers* 25 (1958): 135-42.

[2] Eli Heckscher, "The Effect of Foreign Trade on the Distribution of Income,'
in *Readings in International Trade*, ed. H. S. Ellis and Lloyd Metzler (Philadelphia: Blakiston, 1949), pp. 272-300; Ohlin, *Trade*, chap. 2.

[3] Ohlin, *Trade*, p. 63.   [4] Ibid., p. 5.

effect, increase the amounts of the scarce resources in the region
and thereby decrease local demand for and, hence, local wages of
scarce resources.[1] Since a more or less converse pattern of resource use occurs in the regions where different resources are
relatively scarce or abundant, production and trade create a tendency towards the equalization of factor prices across the system of
regions.[2]

For given endowments of factors, the tendency toward factor
price equalization will eventually result in the equalization of
comparative costs across regions, as relative scarcities and abundances of factors become the same in all regions. Thus production
and trade tend to eliminate comparative advantage, and the division
of production among regions is no longer determined by relative
costs.[3] Both Heckscher and Ohlin, however, discount the possibility
of this geographical indeterminacy of production by expanding their
analyses to cover time-periods long enough to allow endowments to be
replenished in response to increased production resulting from trade.
The original inequalities in resource endowments cause production of
goods intensive in the abundant factors, thereby causing the relative
prices of these factors to rise. These increased factor prices, in
turn, call forth still greater supplies of the already abundant
factors; so comparative costs in production continue to be functions
of comparative factor endowments.[4]

Cost Advantage versus Physical Advantage

Although Heckscher and Ohlin differ from Ricardo in relating
factor endowment proportions to comparative advantage, they retain
the essentially Ricardian notion of comparative advantage as cost
advantage. That is, they derive comparative advantage from factor
endowments via the intermediate connection of relative endowments
with relative factor prices. Samuelson, however, proves that in a
region which sells its output in interregional and world markets,
production costs can be determined independently of factor endowments. With constant returns to scale and intraregional factor
mobility, each factor price ratio can be uniquely related to an output price ratio. Even before the equalization of relative scarcities
and abundances envisioned by Heckscher and Ohlin, factor prices

---

[1]Heckscher, "Effect of Trade," p. 279.   [2]Ohlin, Trade, p. 66.

[3]Heckscher, "Effect of Trade," p. 286.

[4]Ibid., p. 293; Ohlin, Trade, p. 81.

may be equalized and the geographic pattern of production may become indeterminate with regard to costs.[1] Hence, in an interregional trading system, resource endowments cannot necessarily be linked to comparative advantage via an intermediate effect of factor prices.

Jones suggests an alternative to the cost definition of comparative advantage that preserves the essential Heckscher-Ohlin insight into the importance of relative factor endowments: if two regions were producing two goods in the same proportion, the region with the relatively larger physical endowment of a certain factor would be able to expand production of the good intensive in the abundant factor at a lower opportunity cost. Comparative advantage can therefore be construed as a bias towards production of commodities intensive in the use of factors of which the region has relatively abundant physical endowments.[2]

For instance, in a two commodity, two-factor interregional system, even if regions face the same output prices and unit production costs under constant returns to scale, full employment of factors requires that a region must produce relatively larger quantities of the good that is intensive in the region's relatively abundant factor.[3] Jones's modification of the Heckscher-Ohlin theory

---

[1] Paul A. Samuelson, "International Factor Price Equalization Once Again," Economic Journal 59 (June 1949): 181-97.

[2] Ronald W. Jones, "Factor Proportions and the Heckscher-Ohlin Theorem," Review of Economic Studies 24 (1956-57): 1-10.

[3] Assuming constant returns, the full-employment effect of factor endowments on output ratios can be demonstrated for two goods, x_1 and x_2, manufactured by a region endowed with two factors in the ratio $\bar{y}_1/\bar{y}_2$. Let a_{ij} be the coefficient of production of good j for factor i, and let $\rho_j = a_{1j}/a_{2j}$ be the factor intensity ratio of good j. Then full employment requires:

$$a_{11}x_1 + a_{12}x_2 = \bar{y}_1$$
$$a_{21}x_1 + a_{22}x_2 = \bar{y}_2 \quad \text{or} \quad \frac{a_{11}}{\rho_1}x_1 + \frac{a_{12}}{\rho_2}x_2 = \frac{\bar{y}_1}{(\bar{y}_1/\bar{y}_2)}$$

i.e.,

$$\begin{bmatrix} a_{11} & a_{12} \\ a_{11}/\rho_1 & a_{12}/\rho_2 \end{bmatrix} \begin{bmatrix} x_1 \\ x_2 \end{bmatrix} = \begin{bmatrix} \underline{A} \end{bmatrix} \begin{bmatrix} x_1 \\ x_2 \end{bmatrix} = \begin{bmatrix} \bar{y}_1 \\ \bar{y}_1/(\bar{y}_1/\bar{y}_2) \end{bmatrix}.$$

Hence:

$$(*) \quad \frac{x_1}{x_2} = \frac{(a_{12}\bar{y}_1/|\underline{A}|)\,(1/\rho_2 - 1/(\bar{y}_1/\bar{y}_2))}{(a_{11}\bar{y}_1/|\underline{A}|)\,(1/(\bar{y}_1/\bar{y}_2) - 1/\rho_1)} = \frac{a_{22}((\bar{y}_1/\bar{y}_2) - \rho_2)}{a_{12}(\rho_1 - (\bar{y}_1/\bar{y}_2))}$$

See Miltiades Chacholiades, International Trade Theory and Policy (New York:

of factor endowments attributes the geographic pattern of production directly to the geographic pattern of physical resources, without relying on an intermediate connection between physical quantities and resource prices.

Summary of Trade and Location

While Weber attributes geographic differences in locational pull to differences in resource costs, Ohlin attributes the costs themselves to geographic differences in factor endowments and thereby places the locational pull mechanism in a larger context wherein it is an effect as well as a cause of the pattern of industrial location. Ohlin's theory possesses the Ricardian virtue of deriving regional output proportions from finite and immobile resource endowments along with the Weberian virtue of decomposing locational advantage into geographically determined components. Indeed, Ponsard sees Weber's idea of the localization of industries according to comparative input and marketing costs as a sort of prolegomenon to the theories of market and regional interdependence propounded by Ohlin.[1]

Weber predicts which location will produce given goods while Heckscher and Ohlin predict which goods will be produced by given locations. Together, the Weber least-cost location model and the Heckscher-Ohlin factor endowments model comprise a broad theoretical apparatus for analyzing patterns of industrial geography, both within and among regions. The next chapter presents a more rigorous and technical formulation of this intra- and interregional apparatus in order to show that particular elements of the least-cost location model can be identified as logical and functional counterparts of particular elements of the factor endowments model.

McGraw-Hill, 1978), p. 248.

Under conditions of factor price equalization, a_{12}, a_{22}, ρ_1, and ρ_2 will be the same in all regions. Therefore, the ratio of outputs, x_1/x_2, will vary interregionally as the ratio of endowments, $\bar{y}_1/\bar{y}_2$, varies. For example, if region A is relatively abundant in factor 1 compared to region B, then $(\bar{y}_1/\bar{y}_2)^A$ will be closer to ρ_1 and farther from ρ_2 than $(\bar{y}_1/\bar{y}_2)^B$ will be. By equation (*), region A will produce a relatively larger amount of x_1, the good that uses its abundant factor intensity.

[1] Claude Ponsard, Économie et èspace (Paris: École Pratique des Hautes Études, 1955), p. 301.

CHAPTER III

DUALITY: A COMBINED TRADE AND

LOCATION MODEL

A foundation for a trade-theoretic model of location lies in
the correspondence between Ohlin's trade theory and Weber's location
theory. Isard states that "trade and location are as two sides of
the same coin,"[1] but he provides no concrete demonstration of the
aptness of such a simile. This chapter endeavors to demonstrate that
a duality exists between modified versions of Weber's least-cost
location model and the factor endowments model of Heckscher-Ohlin
trade theory. Weber's location theory is modified to include
Thünen's analysis of site rent and Moses's analysis of variable factor
proportions.[2] Henceforth, this version of a least-cost location
model is labelled W-T-M. The Heckscher-Ohlin theory is interpreted
according to Jones's definition of comparative advantage as a production bias arising from factor endowments.[3] Henceforth, this
version of a factor endowments model is labelled H-O-J.

Demonstrating the duality of W-T-M and H-O-J requires two main
assumptions: (1) Weber's assumption that producers face given, fixed
output prices and (2) Heckscher's and Ohlin's assumption that resources are immobile between regions. In particular, assuming fixed
prices and immobile resources makes it possible to prove that a
nonlinear programming formulation of the Weber-Thünen-Moses model
(W-T-M) is the dual of a nonlinear programming formulation of the
Heckscher-Ohlin-Jones model (H-O-J). That is, if there is a solution
to the factor endowments (H-O-J) program, then there is also a
solution to the least-cost location (W-T-M) program; so location
theory is indeed the other side of the coin from trade theory.

---

[1]Isard, Location, p. 207.

[2]Weber, Location of Industries; Thünen, Isolated State; Moses, "Location
and Production."

[3]Heckscher, "Effect of Trade"; Ohlin, Trade; R. Jones, "Factor Proportions."

Assumptions of the Trade/Location Model

Weber's model is based on a partial equilibrium approach that takes output prices as given in order to explain the location of production without further complicating the model with explanations of market location.[1] Since most of the analysis is from the standpoint of an individual plant, it is reasonable for it to treat plants as price-takers in large markets. Heckscher's and Ohlin's models, on the other hand, seek to explain output prices as well as the location of production. Output (and input) prices are the results as well as the causes of industrial location in a system of interdependent markets.[2] Nevertheless, the assumption of fixed output prices is quite compatible with a Heckscher-Ohlin trade theory if the trading (i.e., producing) regions are taken to be so economically small as to be unable to influence national (or international) prices at any level of output.[3]

Since this is an essay on location theory rather than on trade per se, it should be pointed out that holding the demand facing each region constant in the form of fixed output prices permits trade theory to work as a theory of production location without incurring the additional burden of explaining why a region exports some of its output instead of consuming it at home. Therefore, in contrast to many models of comparative advantage that treat prices as endogenous,[4] this essay will henceforth treat producing regions as if they are small enough with respect to their output markets to be price-takers.

In the matter of factor mobility, there is some conflict between Weber and Heckscher-Ohlin because the former assumes, plausibly, that different locations may share and compete for common resources supplies. As long as "locations" are sub-regional areas within a common region, Weber is compatible with Ohlin, whose intraregional location theory is based on Thünen and Weber anyway.[5] For inter-

---

[1] Moses, in "Location and Production," also concentrates on the supply side, although he does offer a cursory treatment of a market with a less than perfectly elastic demand schedule.

[2] Weber holds market prices and locations constant for analytical simplicity, but he also recognizes the interdependence of the space-economy: "each locational distribution of industry, merely by distributing the labor forces, distributes the consumption of industrial products and all other products" (Location of Industries, p. 38).

[3] See, e.g., Richard E. Caves and Ronald W. Jones, World Trade and Payments, 2d ed. (Boston: Little, Brown & Co., 1977), Supplement to chap. 7.

[4] For example, Brian Hindley, The Theory of International Trade (London: Gray-Mills, 1974) or Chacholiades, International Trade, chaps. 2 and 3.

[5] Ohlin, Trade, chap. 10.

regional analysis, though, a clear distinction among regions and their respective production possibilities is necessary; this can be achieved by segregating regional resource supplies. In order to demonstrate a duality between the Weber and factor endowments approaches, at both the interregional and intraregional levels, it is useful to follow Heckscher and Ohlin in imposing interregional immobility, along with intraregional mobility, of resources.[1] Of course, to assure realistic production possibilities, endowments of these resources must be considered during a time-span in which they can plausibly be assumed to be in finite, inelastic supply.

Ohlin is well aware that such an assumption can "tell only part of the story." The supply of factors responds to the demand for factors resulting from production and trade. Therefore supply should only be considered inelastic for the time-span in which the production or migration of factors are unlikely. Moreover, factors can most plausibly be considered immobile if regions are defined as areas within which there is mobility but between which there are large obstacles to movement (e.g., physical distance).[2] In the intranational framework of the models in this essay, the assumption of immobility is probably more supportable with regard to plant and raw materials than labor or financial capital.

Factor Endowments (H-O-J) and Least Cost Location (W-T-M) as Models of Optimization

The duality between the Weberian theory of the locational pull of resources (i.e., the W-T-M model) and the factor endowments hypothesis of Ohlin's trade theory (i.e., the H-O-J model) follows from the fact that both models can be said to treat the geographic pattern of production as resulting from an optimization process whereby the economic system chooses among locations on the basis of geographic data that are, for the time-span of the models, unchangeable and exogenous: input supplies available in the region and output prices received by the region.

H-O-J: Gains from Trade

Heckscher and Ohlin analyze the gains from trade that can

---

[1] It should be noted that Ohlin (Trade, p. 115) drops the assumption of resource immobility for much of his discussion, while Emerson, Location and the Automotive Agreement, assumes interregional immobility of resources in an otherwise Weber-Moses approach to location costs.

[2] Ohlin, Trade, chap. 12.

result if each region produces according to its comparative advantage.[1] Thus the factor endowments model of location (H-O-J) that is embedded in their overall theory depicts a process wherein each region maximizes its gains from trade by maximizing the value of its output (prices x quantities), given the constraints of its limited resource endowments: "each region is best equipped to produce the goods that require large proportions of the factors relatively abundant there."[2] Since output prices are assumed to be exogenously given by world markets, the only variables the region can choose in order to maximize the value of output are the physical quantities and proportions of the goods. H-O-J predicts that the exogenously given proportions in which factors are available will, in conjunction with the available technology,[3] determine in which physical proportions goods should be produced in order to achieve maximum value at given prices.

W-T-M: Wages and Site Rent

The main objective of the least-cost location model (W-T-M) is minimization of total cost (input wages x input amounts) for a given level of output. For a plant facing given demand "to deliver a fixed number of units of product . . . the optimum location . . . is the point at which total expenditure is a minimum."[4] With no barriers to entry of new plants and with competitive factor markets in which individual plants cannot affect wages in the region, this total minimization is subject to the marginal constraints of given output prices. At the equilibrium output levels of the region, the sum of all wages paid to factors for the production of the marginal units[5] should not be less than the unit prices as determined by national (or international) markets. Otherwise, some factors are not being paid the value of their marginal productivity, and new plants should enter the market to garner some of the profits, thereby bidding up the wages of the inelastically supplied factors. These

---

[1]Heckscher, "Effect of Trade," p. 275; Ohlin, _Trade_, p. 28.

[2]Ohlin, _Trade_, p. 7.

[3]Ohlin (ibid., p. 310) implicitly assumes that all regions have access to the same technological knowledge. Weber (_Location of Industries_, pp. 21ff.) considers productivity and, implicitly, technology to be "social" rather than "pure" characteristics of location; and he therefore does not discuss them directly.

[4]Moses, "Location and Production," p. 264.

[5]The marginal unit of output is the one whose production brings industry supply into equality with industry demand, i.e., when the industry's marginal cost equals the (herein, constant) marginal revenue it receives.

<u>marginal</u> constraints do not prevent there arising surplus revenues
on the infra-marginal units of output; so that <u>total</u> regional revenues may exceed the minimized <u>total</u> costs.[1]

In the spatial context of W-T-M, infra-marginal surpluses
occur when given output prices are high enough that even plants located such that their costs are higher than the Weber-Moses minimum
can afford to produce without incurring negative income. In that
case, the lower are a plant's costs due to transport, labor, or
externalities "savings," the further from the margin are the units
it produces. For the region as a whole--i.e., regarding all plants
in all industries as a single aggregate--the situation can be viewed
as one of decreasing returns to scale in the aggregate net income
function of the region. The doubling of variable inputs such as
labor, capital, and raw materials will not double net income, even
though output levels are assumed not to influence output prices.
This is because of the existence of a fixed factor implicit in the
model but not included among the explicitly specified variable factors of the revenue and resource functions: site or production capacity at the site.[2] Greater regional output (and revenue) therefore
requires operation of more of the less well-located plants, which
necessitates (1) drawing more of the variable inputs away from production of final goods and into production of transport services and
(2) receiving fewer boosts to factor productivity from agglomeration
economies.

The result of the decreasing returns due to location is the
creation of economic rent that can be claimed as site rent by landlords.[3] At the limit, where all the rent is extracted as the competition of many plants bids up the rental price of a site, plants
will find no advantage in locating at one site rather than another.
Up to that limit,[4] however, there will be an incentive to locate so
as to minimize costs and earn surplus revenue for a given level of

output.

---

[1]See Paul Samuelson, <u>Foundations of Economic Analysis</u> (Cambridge: Harvard
University Press, 1947), pp. 81-87.

[2]See Tjalling C. Koopmans, <u>Three Essays on the State of Economic Science</u>
(New York: McGraw-Hill, 1957), p. 65.

[3]See, e.g., James M. Henderson and Richard E. Quandt, <u>Microeconomic Theory</u>,
2d. ed. (New York: McGraw-Hill, 1971), pp. 120-21.

[4]Samuelson (<u>Foundations</u>, pp. 85-87) demonstrates that the disposition of
the residual profit, whether it is caused by returns to scale or something else,
will depend on the organization of the market and the degree of freedom of entry
into it.

Since W-T-M assumes that available input amounts are fixed in each region, the only variables that the model allows the economic system to choose in the process of minimizing expenditures (for given output levels and prices) are the input wages in each region.

We have to find, obviously, those elements of cost which differ according to the location of the productive process. If we can secure them, we have the regional factors of location. . . . "Locational factors" are, according to our definition, "advantages in cost." They depend upon the place to which industry goes, and therefore pull industry hither and thither.[1]

Industries will choose a region on the basis of its factor wages in comparison with the wages in other regions. The wages, which reflect the factors' uses in the production of transport as well as final goods, determine an operating cost that in turn dictates how much rent a plant can afford to pay for a location. Moreover, when the W-T-M theory of locational pull is extrapolated to the general equilibrium context addressed by H-O-J, the economic system also has industries "choosing" a region's wages by bidding for the inelastically supplied resources.[2]

Nonlinear Programming Formulation of the Duality Between the H-O-J and W-T-M Models

The implicit duality between H-O-J and W-T-M can be made explicit by putting both models into a nonlinear programming format.

H-O-J: Maximizing the Value of Output[3]

An H-O-J model for two final outputs, two primary inputs, and two regions[4] can be represented by maximizing the objective function in equation (1) subject to the constraints in inequalities (2)-(6).

---

[1] Weber, Location of Industries, p. 25.

[2] Ohlin, Trade, p. 91.

[3] Lefeber (Allocation, chap. 5) and Michael D. Intriligator, Mathematical Optimization and Economic Theory (Englewood Cliffs, N.J.: Prentice-Hall, 1971), chap. 9, sect. 2 give examples of mathematical programming maximization of welfare through maximization of the value of output. The rigorous justification of output maximization derives from the theorem of welfare economics that shows a competitive equilibrium to be a Pareto optimum (see, e.g., Intriligator, Optimization, chap. 10).

[4] The 2-by-2-by-2 model can, without any new assumptions or computational techniques, be generalized to higher dimensions.

$$\text{Max}_{x} \quad \pi(x) = f^1(x_1^1, x_2^1) + f^2(x_1^2, x_2^2) \tag{1}$$

subject to
$$g_1^1(x_1^1, x_2^1) \leq \overline{y}_1^1 \tag{2}$$

$$g_2^1(x_1^1, x_2^1) \leq \overline{y}_2^1 \tag{3}$$

$$g_1^2(x_1^2, x_2^2) \leq \overline{y}_1^2 \tag{4}$$

$$g_2^2(x_1^2, x_2^2) \leq \overline{y}_2^2 \tag{5}$$

$$x_1^k \geq 0, \quad x_2^k \geq 0, \quad k = 1,2 \tag{6}$$

where

$x_j^k \equiv$ amount of final good j produced by region k

$f^k(\cdot) \equiv$ total revenue function of region k

$\overline{y}_i^k \equiv$ fixed endowment of variable factor i available in region k

$g_i^k(\cdot) \equiv$ total amount of factor i used to produce x_1 and x_2 in

region k.

The $f^k(\cdot)$ embody the technological knowledge of the region, the given national (or international) output prices facing the region, and the distances between the region and national (or international) market points.[1] The $g_i^k(\cdot)$ embody the technology of the region, the accessibility of agglomeration economies at potential production sites, and the intraregional distances among given resource sites[2] and potential production sites. These specifications allow for variable factor proportions in production, as assumed by Heckscher, Ohlin, and, importantly, Moses in his extension of Weberian theory.[3]

The geography of a region affects the demand for transport services, since inputs must be moved from source to plant and outputs, given perfectly elastic demand, must absorb transport costs to market. Some writers regard transport only from the standpoint of derived demand, i.e., as an input into the production of final goods.[4] Samuelson, however, points out that transport services are

---

[1] For measuring market distances, all production locations within the same region are taken to be at the region's geographical center or some other common base point.

[2] Following Weber (Location of Industries, pp. 37-38), the geographic sources of inputs are assumed given. This does not contradict Ohlin (Trade, chap. 10), whose interregional location theory is based on Thünen and Weber.

[3] Heckscher, "Effect of Trade"; Ohlin, Trade, p. 64; Moses, "Location and Production."

[4] See, e.g., Isard, Location or Curtis C. Harris and Frank E. Hopkins, Locational Analysis (Lexington, Mass.: Lexington Books, 1972).

themselves outputs and, therefore, resources used to produce them are drawn away from the production of final goods.[1]

The $f^k(\cdot)$ and $g_i^k(\cdot)$ are assumed to be, respectively, concave and convex functions. By virtue of the fact that the $g_i^k(\cdot)$ reflect production at different sites within the region affording different degrees of agglomeration economies and requiring different amounts of transport services in order to produce the same amount of output, concavity-convexity means that the program in relations (1)-(6) allows decreasing returns to scale[2] in the production of final goods due to the fixed factor of location. The doubling of regional output requires more than the doubling of variable inputs: providing the increased plant capacity necessitates producing at locations that offer fewer agglomeration benefits to boost the productivity of variable inputs as well as locations that lie at greater distances from the input endowments and thereby require using proportionately more inputs just to produce transportation of the inputs to plants.

The $f^k(\cdot)$ are assumed to be differentiable in x_j^k. The function $\pi(x)$, being a linear combination of concave and differentiable functions, is also concave and differentiable in x_j^k. The $g_i^k(\cdot)$ are assumed to be differentiable in x_j^k. Form the Lagrangean expression (7), where the v_i^k are Lagrange multipliers.[3] Then the preceding assumptions, along with the first-order conditions (8)-(15), are, by the Kuhn-Tucker Theorem, sufficient to guarantee the existence of $\bar{\bar{x}}_j^k$ and $\bar{\bar{v}}_i^k$ such that $\pi(\bar{x})$ is a global maximum.[4]

$$L(x,v) = \pi(x) + \sum_k \sum_i v_i^k [\bar{y}_i^k - g_i^k(x_1^k, x_2^k)] \tag{7}$$

$$\frac{\partial L}{\partial x_1^1} = \frac{\partial f^1}{\partial x_1^1} - v_1^1\frac{\partial g_1^1}{\partial x_1^1} - v_2^1\frac{\partial g_2^1}{\partial x_1^1} \le 0, \ x_1^1 \ge 0, \ x_1^1\frac{\partial L}{\partial x_1^1} = 0 \tag{8}$$

$$\frac{\partial L}{\partial x_2^1} = \frac{\partial f^1}{\partial x_2^1} - v_1^1\frac{\partial g_1^1}{\partial x_2^1} - v_2^1\frac{\partial g_2^1}{\partial x_2^1} \le 0, \ x_2^1 \ge 0, \ x_2^1\frac{\partial L}{\partial x_2^1} = 0 \tag{9}$$

---

[1]Paul A. Samuelson, "The Transfer Problem and Transport Costs" in Readings in International Economics, ed. Richard E. Caves and Harry G. Johnson (Homewood, Ill.: R. D. Irwin, 1968), pp. 115-47.

[2]M. L. Balinski and William J. Baumol, "The Dual in Nonlinear Programming and Its Economic Interpretation," Review of Economic Studies 35 (July 1968): 237-56.

[3]Akira Takayama, Mathematical Economics (Hinsdale, Ill.: Dryden Press, 1974), chap. 1 explains convexity-concavity conditions and the use of Lagrange multipliers to solve nonlinear programming problems.

[4]Balinski and Baumol, "Dual in Nonlinear Programming."

$$\frac{\partial L}{\partial x_1^2} = \frac{\partial f^2}{\partial x_1^2} - v_1^2 \frac{\partial^2 g_1}{\partial x_1^2} - v_2^2 \frac{\partial^2 g_2}{\partial x_1^2} \leq 0, \ x_1^2 \geq 0, \ x_1^2 \frac{\partial L}{\partial x_1^2} = 0 \qquad (10)$$

$$\frac{\partial L}{\partial x_2^2} = \frac{\partial f^2}{\partial x_2^2} - v_1^2 \frac{\partial^2 g_1}{\partial x_2^2} - v_2^2 \frac{\partial^2 g_2}{\partial x_2^2} \leq 0, \ x_2^2 \geq 0, \ x_2^2 \frac{\partial L}{\partial x_2^2} = 0 \qquad (11)$$

$$\frac{\partial L}{\partial v_1^1} = \bar{y}_1^1 - g_1^1(x_1^1, x_2^1) \geq 0, \ v_1^1 \geq 0, \ v_1^1 \frac{\partial L}{\partial v_1^1} = 0 \qquad (12)$$

$$\frac{\partial L}{\partial v_2^1} = \bar{y}_2^1 - g_2^1(x_1^1, x_2^1) \geq 0, \ v_2^1 \geq 0, \ v_2^1 \frac{\partial L}{\partial v_2^1} = 0 \qquad (13)$$

$$\frac{\partial L}{\partial v_1^2} = \bar{y}_1^2 - g_1^2(x_1^2, x_2^2) \geq 0, \ v_1^2 \geq 0, \ v_1^2 \frac{\partial L}{\partial v_1^2} = 0 \qquad (14)$$

$$\frac{\partial L}{\partial v_2^2} = \bar{y}_2^2 - g_2^2(x_1^2, x_2^2) \geq 0, \ v_2^2 \geq 0, \ v_2^2 \frac{\partial L}{\partial v_2^2} = 0 \qquad (15)$$

Thus the H-O-J program describes the maximization of the value of output by an interregional system, $\pi(x)$, subject to fixed factor endowments, $\bar{y}_i^k$, as in Heckscher-Ohlin trade theory. The program's solution, $\bar{x}_j^k$, is the amount of good j production that should be located in region k. Of course, this representation of the industrial location process is highly stylized in order to illuminate the general relationships among geography, technology, and prices. There is insufficient detail in the program's specification for it to be used as an actual instrument for allocating production in space.[1]

H-O-J and W-T-M Connected by Wages

Complementary slackness in conditions (12)-(15) requires that the Lagrange multipliers v_i^k equal zero whenever not all of the endowment of factor i is used up in production in region k, but that v_i^k should be positive whenever the endowment is exhausted. This

---

[1]Cf. Lefeber, Allocation; Serck-Hanssen, Optimal Location; George G. Judge and Takashi Takayama, eds., Studies in Economic Planning over Space and Time (Amsterdam: North-Holland Publishing Co., 1973).

suggests that v may be the marginal value of the scarce resource
i in region k at the Kuhn-Tucker maximum of output value. Indeed,
Balinski and Baumol prove:

$$\frac{\partial \bar{\bar{\pi}}}{\partial \bar{Y}_i^k} = v_i^k \tag{16}$$

where $\bar{\pi}$ is the maximum output value expressed as a function of
regional factor endowments.[1]

In other words, v_i^k is the marginal increase in $\bar{\pi}$ when region
k's endowment of factor i is increased by one unit. (The magnitude
of v_i^k must reflect the fact that increasing the magnitude of output
requires dedicating some of the increased factor supply to the production of the intermediate good transport.) Hence the nonlinear
programming solution of H-O-J for amounts (and proportions) of outputs also computes the optimal wages of inputs. The v_i^k are the
costs of each factor in each region chosen (imputed) by an optimizing
force (the free market with perfect information or an omniscient
planner).

Now the W-T-M model, too, is concerned with optimal factor
wages in each region. These wages define the optimal locational
pull of each region and thereby imply where plants should locate,
and with what capacity, in order to achieve overall cost minimization
with regard to a particular level of output by an interregional
system. For this reason, equation (16) implies the fundamental
connection between the nonlinear programs of H-O-J and W-T-M.

W-T-M: Minimizing Expenditures and Site Rent

If the input wages "chosen" by an optimizing economic system
as industries minimize expenditures can be shown to equal those
wages "chosen" as regions determine output amounts (and proportions),
then a duality between H-O-J and W-T-M will be revealed. The nonlinear programming dual[2] to the primal (H-O-J) program in equation
(1) and inequalities (2)-(6) is the constrained minimization in
equation (17) and inequalities (18)-(22).[3]

---

[1] Balinski and Baumol, "Dual in Nonlinear Programming," sect. 3.

[2] The dual of the dual is not the primal.

[3] Balinski and Baumol, "Dual in Nonlinear Programming."

$$\text{Minimize}_{x,v} \quad \alpha(x,v) = \Sigma\Sigma v_i^k \, \overline{y}_i^k + [\pi(x) - \Sigma\Sigma v_i^k g_i^k (x_1^k, x_2^k)]$$
$$ {}_{ki} {}_{ki}$$

$$- \Sigma\Sigma x_j^k (\frac{\partial f^k}{\partial x_j^k} - \Sigma v_i^k \frac{\partial g_i^k}{\partial x_j^k}) \qquad (17)$$
$${}_{kj} {}_{i}$$

$$\text{subject to} \quad v_1^1 \frac{\partial g_1^1}{\partial x_1^1} + v_2^1 \frac{\partial g_2^1}{\partial x_1^1} \geq \frac{\partial f^1}{\partial x_1^1} \qquad (18)$$

$$v_1^1 \frac{\partial g_1^1}{\partial x_2^1} + v_2^1 \frac{\partial g_2^1}{\partial x_2^1} \geq \frac{\partial f^1}{\partial x_2^1} \qquad (19)$$

$$v_1^2 \frac{\partial g_1^2}{\partial x_1^2} + v_2^2 \frac{\partial g_2^2}{\partial x_1^2} \geq \frac{\partial f^2}{\partial x_1^2} \qquad (20)$$

$$v_1^2 \frac{\partial g_1^2}{\partial x_2^2} + v_2^2 \frac{\partial g_2^2}{\partial x_2^2} \geq \frac{\partial f^2}{\partial x_2^2} \qquad (21)$$

$$v_1^k \geq 0, \; v_2^k \geq 0, \; k = 1,2 \qquad (22)$$

Assuming that the x_j^k have already been selected so as to maximize the primal objective function--i.e., assuming $x_j^k = \overline{x}_j^k$--then the choice variables in the dual are the v_i^k. By the saddle point property of a Kuhn-Tucker solution to a nonlinear program, the x_j^k and v_i^k which maximize the primal will also minimize the dual.[1] By equation (16), the same optimized v_i^k in both primal and dual will be the optimal wages of the scarce inputs (assuming exhaustion of input endowments). Thus the dual program in equation (17) and inequalities (18)-(22) chooses wages for the given regional factor supplies, $\overline{y}_i^k$, so as to minimize total expenditures, $\Sigma v_i^k \overline{y}_i^k$, with respect to given levels (and proportions) of output, $\overline{x}_j^k$. This is similar to the way W-T-M has industries locate so as to minimize total costs with respect to a given level of output.[2]

---

[1] Balinski and Baumol, "Dual in Nonlinear Programming," p. 238.

[2] The claim of similarity between Weber-Moses location decisions and the overall regional factor income minimization process is based on a version of the standard assumption of competitive equilibrium models; individual decision-makers (herein, locators) have perfect information, i.e., the optimal output level (and plant capacity) is known before deciding where to locate. The solution to the

26

In the dual, as in W-T-M, the minimization of costs is constrained by given markets and prices for outputs. This is reflected
in the constraints (18)-(21),[1] which are, for given technology,
functions of the national (or international) prices and of regions'
geographies as embodied in the $f^k(\cdot)$ and $g_i^k(\cdot)$. At the Kuhn-
Tucker minimum, $\partial f^k/\partial x_j^k$ equals the marginal revenue received by
region k for the last, or equilibrium unit of good j produced.
It is essentially the national price of good j discounted by the
costs of transporting the unit of output to market. Since some
inputs are used to provide transport to national (or international)
market locations, some of the revenue received for output is lost
to the producers of transport services. Hence, $\partial f^k/\partial x_j^k$ is the unit
price actually received by the producers of output.

At the same time, the incremental amount of input i required
to produce the marginal unit of output j, $\partial g_i^k/\partial x_j^k$, reflects the
diversion of some inputs to the production of intraregional trans-
port. Constraints (18)-(21) require that wages v_i^k be chosen so
that the $\partial g_i^k/\partial x_j^k$ are paid, in sum, no less than the received prices
of the output units. If the sum of input payments per marginal
output unit is less than the received price, $\partial f^k/\partial x_j^k$, then some
factors are not being paid equilibrium values of their marginal
products and new plants should enter the regional market to bid up
wages.

Since the optimal choice of v_i^k resulting from the minimization
of $\Sigma v_i^k \bar{y}_i^k$ is constrained by the received prices and transport geography of each region, the first term of equation (17) along with
constraints (18)-(22) seem to depict a W-T-M location process.
However, no account has yet been made of site rent; and there are
two other terms in equation (17) that have not been explained.

The last term in equation (17) can be explained by considering the Lagrangean expression that corresponds to the dual
program:[2]

$$L'(x,v,\lambda) = \pi(x) + \sum_{ki}\Sigma v_i^k[\bar{y}_i^k - g_i^k(x_1^k, x_2^k)] + \sum_{kj}\Sigma x_j^k\lambda_j^k \qquad (23)$$

---

primal program yields the optimal level for the industry as a whole, but the
levels for individual competitive plants must be determined by some sort of
"bidding" process (see, e.g., Henderson and Quandt, Microeconomic Theory, chap. 4).

[1]Constraints (18)-(21) are identical to parts of the first-order conditions
(8)-(11) in the primal.

[2]Balinski and Baumol, "Dual in Nonlinear Programming," p. 246.

where $\lambda_j^k = \Sigma v_i^k \dfrac{\partial g_i^k}{\partial x_j^k} - \dfrac{\partial f^k}{\partial x_j^k}$.

By complementary slackness, the last term of equation (23) will equal zero whenever $x_j^k > 0$ for all j and k, i.e., whenever something of each good is produced in each region. In that case, $\Sigma v_i^k \partial g_i^k / \partial x_j^k = \partial f^k / \partial x_j^k$. Constraints (18)-(21) then become equations, which ensures that the received unit prices will exactly cover the payments to factors and no opportunity loss will result from producing at the Kuhn-Tucker optimum levels.

In contrast to the last term, the second term of equation (17) will not, in general, disappear, even when factors are paid their marginal value products and something of each good is produced. This is because the second term embodies whatever "savings" accrue to producers of the infra-marginal units of output due to transport or agglomeration economies. When resources are fully employed and optimally allocated so that their wages, v_i^k, reflect their value in production (of transport as well as final goods), producers any-where in the same region will face the same wages under the assump-tion of intraregional factor mobility. Yet, because not all pro-duction sites will necessarily be optimally located in a Weber-Moses (least-cost) sense, some plants will pay higher transport costs or receive fewer agglomeration benefits than other plants. For example, the plants farther from sources of labor will pay higher labor transport costs, perhaps in the form of a wage premium to cover the workers' costs of commuting. The better-located producers will have surplus revenue with which to pay higher rents for their sites, as in the process analyzed by Thünen. Hence, the term $\pi(x) - \Sigma\Sigma v_i^k g_i^k (x_1^k, x_2^k)$ represents economic rent--or the excess of total revenue, $\pi(x)$, over total payments to factors used, $\Sigma\Sigma v_i^k g_i^k$--when each factor is paid its optimal wage v_i^k.[1]

In summary, when something of each good is produced in each region and site rent is taken into account, the dual program in equation (17) and inequalities (18)-(22) represents a W-T-M process of locating production capacity in all regions. The geography of the regions, along with the minimization of operational and loca-tional costs, $(\Sigma\Sigma v_i^k y_i^k + [\pi(x) - \Sigma\Sigma v_i^k g_i^k])$, determine the cost of production at each site in each region. That is, the v_i^k and the transport distance embodied in the $f^k(\cdot)$ and $g_i^k(\cdot)$ determine the delivered costs of inputs at each site, which imply the <u>isodapanes</u>

---

[1]Balinski and Baumol, "Dual in Nonlinear Programming," p. 246.

of Weber and the iso-outlay curves of Moses.[1] Those plants located
at the minimum cost points indicated by the isolines may pay higher
site rents à la Thünen.

Summary of H-O-J/W-T-M Duality

By the saddle point property of the Kuhn-Tucker solution, the
optimal x_j^k and v_i^k in both the primal and dual programs are identical.
The W-T-M location program (17)-(22) can therefore be said to be the
dual of the H-O-J factor endowments program (1)-(6). Where there is
a solution for the H-O-J problem, there is also one for the W-T-M
problem.[2] The solution of the programming problems will reflect
geographic constraints on the location of industry. The fixed parameters of the primal constraints (2)-(5) are the fixed regional
factor endowments $\bar{y}_i^k$, which are geographic parameters. The fixed
parameters of the dual constraints (18)-(21) are likewise geographic
because the received unit prices $\partial f^k/\partial x_j^k$ are geographically variant
according to the market distances embodied in the $f^k(\cdot)$.

All this strongly suggests that industrial location problems
which assume fixed regional resources and prices can be attacked
with the factor endowments theory of comparative advantage. Holding
regional resources finite and immobile provides a concise and wieldy
criterion for distinguishing among regions on the basis of their
respective production possibilities. Holding the demand facing each
region constant in the form of fixed output prices allows the trade
theory of comparative advantage to be interpreted as a theory of
production location without burdening it with the need to explain
why a region consumes or exports its output in one proportion rather
than another.

By assuming finite, interregionally immobile resources and
fixed commodity price ratios, this essay has been able to demonstrate
that modified versions of Weber's least-cost location model and
Ohlin's factor endowments model are dual approaches to the same basic
location problem. That is, if Weber's model is revised to account
for Thünen's theory of rent and Moses's analysis of variable proportions and if Ohlin's model is interpreted according to Jones's
definition of factor abundance as physical abundance, then the two
approaches to industrial geography are like "two sides of the same
coin."

---

[1] Weber, Location of Industries, p. 102; Moses, "Location and Production,"
p. 262.

[2] Balinski and Baumol, "Dual in Nonlinear Programming," p. 240.

CHAPTER IV

THE GENERAL TRADE/LOCATION MODEL AS A

SPECIFICALLY INTERREGIONAL MODEL

OF INDUSTRIAL LOCATION

This chapter concentrates on those aspects of the general
H-O-J/W-T-M model in chapter III that are specifically concerned
with interregional--as opposed to intraregional--analysis of production locations.

Areal versus Punctual Location Theory

The general model discussed in chapter III embodies two approaches to location problems that are distinguishable more for
their relative emphases than for their basic assumptions. One
approach emphasizes distance as a force behind location patterns
within an area, while the other approach stresses the influence of
differences among geographic points in their predetermined characteristics. The first, or areal, approach to location theory does
take some geographic differences as predetermined; but it primarily
aims at predicting the economic characteristics of places within an
area on the basis of constraints imposed by intra-areal distances,
especially in the form of transport costs. Lösch's derivation of
hexagonal economic areas from a uniform plain, Alonso's bid-rent
function, and Mills's urban model are examples of this areal approach.[1] The second, or punctual, approach to location theory may
account for distance through some provision for transport costs,
but it primarily aims at predicting economic relations among geographic points on the basis of differences in such parameters as
prices, resources, and technology. Samuelson's system of equations
for world-wide general equilibrium, Lefeber's optimal location algorithm, and Emerson's comparison of United States and Canadian
automotive production are examples of this punctual approach.[2]

---

[1]August Lösch, The Economics of Location, trans. from 2d rev. ed. by
William H. Woglam and Wolfgang F. Stolper (New Haven, Conn.: Yale University Press,
1954); Alonso, Location and Land Use; Edwin S. Mills, Studies in the Structure
of the Urban Economy (Baltimore: Johns Hopkins Press, 1972).

[2]Paul A. Samuelson, "Prices of Factors and Goods in General Equilibrium,"

The areal approach to location is used for many of the intra-regional aspects of the H-O-J/W-T-M model. Given resource sites, the rest of the production location pattern within a region is largely a function of transport costs and consequent site rentals. The punctual approach to location is used for many of the inter-regional aspects of the H-O-J/W-T-M model. Transport costs to markets are acknowledged, but the rest of the interregional pattern derives from predetermined differences in resource prices and supplies.

Judging from surveys in Smith, Miller and Jensen, and Brown,[1] most studies of industrial location written from the standpoint of production rather than markets have been intraregional analyses. That is, they have been areal analyses of distance and transport that explain intraregional locations. Indeed, those portions of Ohlin's interregional trade study that do deal with intraregional theory are explicitly drawn from those portions of Thünen's and Weber's works that are areal analyses.[2] Thus the greatest opportunity for trade theory to contribute to industrial location theory may lie in the field of interregional analysis.

According to Böventer, trade theory treats regions as internally homogeneous and regards intraregional movement as costless. In effect, it takes a punctual approach to location that collapses regions into points and then determines the optimal specialization of production among these points.[3] The contribution of trade theory to industrial location theory might, therefore, involve stressing the punctual analyses of the H-O-J/W-T-M model in order to elaborate on its trade-theoretic elements for the analysis of interregional production differences. In particular, two powerful hypotheses are demonstrated to follow from the interregional model. One is that if a region possesses relatively more of a factor than another region, then the abundant region will produce relatively more of the goods that use the abundant factor intensively. The other hypothesis is

Review of Economic Studies 21 (1953-54): 1-20; Lefeber, Allocation; Emerson, Location and the Automotive Agreement.

[1]David M. Smith, Industrial Location (New York: Wiley, 1971); Stephen M. Miller and Oscar W. Jensen, "Location and the Theory of Production: A Review and Critique of Recent Contributions," Regional Science and Urban Economics 8 (1978): 117-28; Douglas M. Brown, "The Location Decision of the Firm: An Overview of Theory and Evidence," Papers, Regional Science Association 43 (1979): 23-39.

[2]Ohlin, Trade; Thünen, Isolated State; Weber, Location of Industry.

[3]E. von Böventer, "Toward a United Theory of Spatial Economic Structure," Papers, Regional Science Association 10 (1963): 163-87.

that if one region absorbs lower transport costs to market (receives
a higher price) than another region, then the region receiving the
higher price will pay a higher relative wage to the factor used intensively in the higher-priced good.

Specializing H-O-J/W-T-M to a
Two-Good Two-Factor Model of
Regional Equilibrium

Under certain simplifying assumptions, the generalized H-O-J/
W-T-M model in relations (1)-(23) of the previous chapter can be
transformed into a special case that underscores the capability of
the punctual approach to location theory for explaining interregional
industrial equilibrium. The constraints (2)-(5) and (18)-(21) can
be made to yield Jones's basic general equilibrium model,[1] provided
that the regional production functions of each industry are assumed
to exhibit constant returns to scale.[2] This implies the elimination
of agglomeration benefits which boost the productivity of inputs as
well as the elimination of the demand for intraregional transport
which draws inputs away from production of final goods. (For
example, a region can be conceived as an area small enough that
intraregional transport costs are negligible next to other costs of
production.) Transport costs to market are retained, but the services are assumed to be provided at constant cost by a third-party
producer of transport who does not draw on the factor supplies of
the regions in the model. Thus transport will not be treated as an
implicit intermediate good, although it was so treated in the previous chapter. Under these conditions, fixed output prices and free
entry into the final goods markets imply there will be no economic
rent nor, in particular, any site rent. Furthermore, per-unit
transport costs to market and, hence, received unit prices will be
constant for all levels of output.

With constant returns to scale, total factor demands for total
output are simple multiples of factor demands for single units of
output. Let a_{ij} be the coefficient of production for the use of

---

[1]R. Jones, "General Equilibrium."

[2]When Weber (Location of Industries, pp. 111 and 227) assumes fixed factor
proportions in discussing production coefficients for labor and raw materials, he
thereby also assumes production functions are homogeneous degree one. When he
discusses agglomeration externalities (pp. 127ff.), his production function that
explicitly contains only labor and raw materials must be assumed to exhibit non-
constant returns at locations affording the externalities. Ohlin (Trade, p. 73),
like Weber, treats economies of scale as a cause of the geographical division of
production; but much of his discussion elsewhere implies constant returns.

factor i in the production of good j: the amount of i required to produce one unit of j. The constraints (2)-(5) relate total amounts of inputs used on total outputs to total available input supplies. Assuming production exhausts all resource endowments, complementary slackness in conditions (12)-(15) permits rewriting the constraints as equations:

$$a_{11}^1 x_1^1 + a_{12}^1 x_2^1 = \bar{y}_1^1 \tag{2'}$$

$$a_{21}^1 x_1^1 + a_{22}^1 x_2^1 = \bar{y}_2^1 \tag{3'}$$

$$a_{11}^2 x_1^2 + a_{12}^2 x_2^2 = \bar{y}_1^2 \tag{4'}$$

$$a_{21}^2 x_1^2 + a_{22}^2 x_2^2 = \bar{y}_2^2 \tag{5'}$$

Since the amount of a factor used for one unit of output is the same at all levels of output under constant returns to scale, the $\partial g_i^k / \partial x_j^k$ in constraints (18)-(21) are constant and, in fact, equal to the appropriate a_{ij}. With transport costs to market constant at all levels, any $\partial f^k / \partial x_j^k$ is also a constant, say, P_j^k: the price of good j <u>received</u> in region k. Assuming something of each good is produced in each region, complementary slackness in conditions (8)-(11) permits rewriting the constraints (18)-(21) as equations:

$$a_{11}^1 v_1^1 + a_{21}^1 v_2^1 = P_1^1 \tag{18'}$$

$$a_{12}^1 v_1^1 + a_{22}^1 v_2^1 = P_2^1 \tag{19'}$$

$$a_{11}^2 v_1^2 + a_{21}^2 v_2^2 = P_1^2 \tag{20'}$$

$$a_{12}^2 v_1^2 + a_{22}^2 v_2^2 = P_2^2 \tag{21'}$$

The linearity of equations (1) and (17), along with the regional division of the constraints (2)-(5) and (18)-(21) implies that the dual objectives of maximization in H-O-J and minimization in W-T-M can be achieved by maximizing and minimizing within each separate regional economy. Equations (2')-(5') and (18')-(21') can therefore be grouped by region to describe two separate regional equilibria in two regions that share a common technology but may have different factor endowments and receive different prices for the same product in the same national (or international) markets.

The activity analysis format of these equations is precisely the one used by Jones to derive the comparative statics properties of general equilibrium when factor endowments and output prices are treated as exogenous parameters and the relative factor intensities of goods are assumed not to reverse for any change in equilibrium factor prices.[1]

The Effect of Endowment Proportions on Output Proportions

Applying Jones's methods to the special case of the H-O-J constraints in equations (2') and (3') or (4') and (5') yields a formula for the effect of a change in one region's resource proportions $\bar{y}_1/\bar{y}_2$ on its output proportions x_1/x_2:[2]

$$\frac{d(\frac{x_1}{x_2})}{(\frac{x_1}{x_2})} = \frac{1}{|\lambda|} \frac{d(\frac{\bar{y}_1}{\bar{y}_2})}{(\frac{\bar{y}_1}{\bar{y}_2})} + \sigma \frac{d(\frac{P_1}{P_2})}{(\frac{P_1}{P_2})}$$

or, equivalently, (24)

$$\frac{dx_1}{x_1} - \frac{dx_2}{x_2} = \frac{1}{|\lambda|} (\frac{dy_1}{y_1} - \frac{d\bar{y}_2}{\bar{y}_2}) + \sigma (\frac{dP_1}{P_1} - \frac{dP_2}{P_2}).$$

The quantity $|\lambda|$ is the determinant of the matrix of transforms of the a_{ij}'s that appear when equations (2') and (3') or (4') and (5') are totally differentiated to derive equations (24): $\lambda_{ij} = a_{ij}x_j/\bar{y}_i$, i.e., the proportion of the region's endowment of factor i that is used up in the production of good j. Since $\lambda_{i1} + \lambda_{i2} = 1$, it must be true that $-1 \leq |\lambda| \leq 1$.

Equations (24) say that if the ratio of output prices is unchanged while there is an increase in the ratio of one factor's endowment to the other factor's endowment, then there will be an even larger proportionate increase in the ratio of the output intensive in the most increased factor to the output intensive in the other factor.[3] If x_1 is intensive in y_1, i.e., good 1 is intensive in

---

[1]R. Jones, "General Equilibrium."

[2]Ibid., p. 563. The superscript denoting region is dropped.

[3]In the case where only one endowment increases while the other is unchanged, equations (24) imply there will be an absolute increase in the commodity intensive in the increased factor and an absolute decrease in the commodity intensive in the unchanged factor (see R. Jones, "General Equilibrium," p. 561). This is the so-called Rybczynski effect. T. M. Rybczynski, "Factor Endowments and Relative Commodity Prices," Economica 22 (November 1955): 336-41.

factor 1 and there are no factor intensity reversals between goods, then $a_{11}a_{22} > a_{12}a_{21}$; and it can be shown that $|\lambda|$ is always <u>positive</u> In that case, equations (24) say that for constant relative output prices,[1] i.e., $dP_1/P_1 - dP_2/P_2 = 0$, the expansion of $\bar{y}_1$ at a greater rate than $\bar{y}_2$ will cause an expansion of x_1 at a greater rate than x_2:

$$\frac{d\bar{y}_1}{\bar{y}_1} - \frac{d\bar{y}_2}{\bar{y}_2} > 0 \stackrel{\rightarrow}{\leftarrow} \frac{dx_1}{x_1} - \frac{dx_2}{x_2} > 0$$

or, equivalently, (25)

$$\frac{d\bar{y}_1}{\bar{y}_1} > \frac{d\bar{y}_2}{\bar{y}_2} \stackrel{\rightarrow}{\leftarrow} \frac{dx_1}{x_1} > \frac{dx_2}{x_2} .$$

When the changes $d\bar{y}_i$ and dx_j are interregional rather than intertemporal, that is, when they denote endowment and output differences between two regions with a common technology receiving the same output prices, then

$$\frac{d\bar{y}_i}{\bar{y}_i} = \frac{\bar{y}_i^1 - \bar{y}_i^2}{\bar{y}_i^1} = 1 - \frac{\bar{y}_i^2}{\bar{y}_i^1} \text{ and } \frac{dx_j}{x_j} = \frac{x_j^1 - x_j^2}{x_j^1} = 1 - \frac{x_j^2}{x_j^1} .$$

Hence, relations (25) become

$$\frac{\bar{y}_1^1}{\bar{y}_2^1} > \frac{\bar{y}_1^2}{\bar{y}_2^2} \stackrel{\rightarrow}{\leftarrow} \frac{x_1^1}{x_2^1} > \frac{x_1^2}{x_2^2}$$ (26)

Relation (26) predicts regional differences in commodity composition of output on the basis of regional differences in relative factor endowments. When $\bar{y}_1^1/\bar{y}_2^1 > \bar{y}_1^2/\bar{y}_2^2$, region 1 is more abundant than region 2 in factor 1. Since relations (24)-(26) have relative factor abundance implying that relatively more output of the good that is intensive in the abundant factor, they reflect Jones's interpretation of the Heckscher-Ohlin theory of the effect of relative factor endowments on the commodity composition of regional output.[2]

---

[1]When prices are not equal across regions--e.g., when transport costs to market cause regions to receive different fractions of the given national (or international) price--then the second terms of equations (24) come into play. The amount σ is the elasticity of transformation of the region's production frontiers. If regions share the same technology, σ measures the degree to which they should alternate production of x_1 with x_2 as different market distances cause relative prices to change across regions.

[2]R. Jones, "Factor Proportions."

The Effect of Received Price Ratios
on Wage Ratios

Samuelson demonstrates that in general equilibrium, the following relationship holds:[1]

$$\frac{\partial x_j}{\partial y_i} = \frac{\partial v_i}{\partial P_j} \tag{27}$$

That is, if an increase (decrease) in the region's endowment of factor i, with prices and all other endowments constant, causes an increase in the output of good j, then an increase in the region's received price for good j, with endowments and all other prices constant, will cause an increase (decrease) in the wage of factor i; and the two changes will be of equivalent sizes, whichever one takes place. This suggests that the factor endowments results (24)-(26) for the H-O-J constraints must have dual received price results for the W-T-M constraints.

Applying Jones's method to the special case of the W-T-M constraints in equations (18') and (19') or (20') and (21') yields a formula for the effect of a change in the relative prices P_1/P_2 received by a region on the relative wages v_1/v_2 of factors in the region:[2]

$$\frac{d(\frac{v_1}{v_2})}{(\frac{v_1}{v_2})} = \frac{1}{|\theta|} \frac{d(\frac{P_1}{P_2})}{(\frac{P_1}{P_2})}$$

or, equivalently   (28)

$$\frac{dv_1}{v_1} - \frac{dv_2}{v_2} = \frac{1}{|\theta|}(\frac{dP_1}{P_1} - \frac{dP_2}{P_2})$$

The quantity $|\theta|$ is the determinant of the matrix of transforms of the a_{ij}'s that appear when equations (18') and (19') or (20') and (21') are totally differentiated to derive equations (28): $\theta_{ij} = a_{ij}v_i/P_j$; i.e., the share of factor i in the total (competitive) cost of producing a unit of good j in the region. By the same

---

[1] Samuelson, "Prices of Factors and Goods." Murray C. Kemp, Three Topics in the Theory of International Trade (Amsterdam: North-Holland Publishing Co., 1976), pp. 82-83, concludes that the number of factors must be at least as great as the number of goods for equation (27) to hold.

[2] R. Jones, " General Equilibrium," p. 563.

kind of reasoning that was previously applied to $|\lambda|$, it must be true that $-1 \le |\theta| \le 1$.

Equations (28) say that if there is a rise in the ratio of one output price to the other price, with endowments constant, then there will be an even larger proportionate increase in the relative wage of the factor used intensively in the output of which the price rises most.[1] If x_1 is intensive in y_1 and there are no factor intensity reversals, then it can be shown that $|\theta|$ is always positive. In that case, equations (28) say that if P_1 increases at a greater rate than P_1, with endowments constant,[2] then v_1 will increase at a greater rate than v_2:

$$\frac{dP_1}{P_1} - \frac{dP_2}{P_2} > 0 \;\vec{\to}\; \frac{dv_1}{v_1} - \frac{dv_2}{v_2} > 0$$

(29)

or, equivalently,

$$\frac{dP_1}{P_1} > \frac{dP_2}{P_2} \;\vec{\to}\; \frac{dv_1}{v_1} > \frac{dv_2}{v_2} \;.$$

When the dP_j and dv_i are interregional differences, i.e., between two regions that face the same markets with the same technology and factor endowment proportions, then

$$\frac{dP_j}{P_j} = \frac{P_j^1 - P_j^2}{P_j^1} = 1 - \frac{P_j^2}{P_j^1} \quad\text{and}\quad \frac{dv_i}{v_i} = \frac{v_i^1 - v_i^2}{v_i^1} = 1 - \frac{v_i^2}{v_i^1} \;.$$

Hence, relations (29) become

$$\frac{P_1^1}{P_2^1} > \frac{P_1^2}{P_2^2} \;\vec{\to}\; \frac{v_1^1}{v_2^1} > \frac{v_1^2}{v_2^2} \;.$$

This wage effect of regional differences in received relative prices reflects the theory of competitive cost minimization, whereby all revenue must be distributed as factor income. Suppose regions

---

[1] In the case where only one commodity price rises while the other remains constant, equations (28) imply that the wage of the factor used intensively in the higher-priced commodity will increase absolutely while the other wage will decrease absolutely (see R. Jones, "General Equilibrium," p. 561). This is the so-called Stolper-Samuelson effect. Wolfgang Stolper and Paul Samuelson, "Protection and Real Wages," Review of Economic Studies 9 (1941): 58-73.

[2] R. Jones ("General Equilibrium") assumes no specialization in a region's production. Otherwise, drastic differences in regional endowments could imply specialization in only one good in an ostensibly two-sector model. Ronald Jones, "The Small Country in a Many-Commodity World," Australian Economic Papers 13 (December 1974): 225-36, discusses the effect of endowments on wages in a multi-sector model.

1 and 2 lie at different distances[1] from the same markets such that $P_1^1/P_2^1 > P_1^2/P_2^2$. Then the unit revenue of good 1 is relatively larger in region 1 than in region 2, which means that the regions' distribution of income will be different. Under constant returns to scale, the higher relative P_1 in region 1 means that relatively more of that region's income must go to the inputs used to produce good 1. It follows that the input used in relatively great amounts--i.e., intensively--in good 1 must benefit most from the higher relative income in the form of a higher relative wage.

The Price-Wage Effect as a Different Perspective on Locational Pull

Relation (30) recalls discussions in previous chapters of general equilibrium insights into Weber's partial equilibrium analysis of locational pull. While regions may exert different pulls because of different "locational factors" or "cost advantages,"[2] these advantages can in large part derive from relative, not absolute, wage levels and so exert relative, not absolute, locational pulls. Depending on relative received prices, relative wages will vary across regions and will thereby be attractive to given industries in varying proportions across regions. In other words, locational pull may be more a matter of the proportions in which industries locate in a region and less a matter of where the absolutely lowest cost production can be located.

What prevents all plants being pulled only to the region or regions offering the absolutely lowest wages are the limited production possibilities of any single region imposed by finite resources combined with fixed received output prices. Any plant capacity or output amount greater than the full-employment equilibrium capacities and amounts implied in equations (2')-(5') will drive the wages of the inelastically supplied factors up, causing equations (18')-(21') to become inequalities, whereby factor payments exceed given prices and it is implied that some plants must cut back production or close down to avoid negative income.

---

[1] The effect on received prices of distance from the market will be greater for those goods for which transport constitutes a larger proportion of the total cost. Hence the magnitude of the wage effect of received prices in result (30) will depend on the physical transport requirements of the goods, as well as on the actual distances to markets.

[2] Weber, Location of Industries, p. 25.

Summary of the Interregional Version
of H-O-J/W-T-M

The areal approach to location theory tends to regard the plant location process as one in which plants seek the best location within an area on the basis of transport distances. The punctual approach is more influenced by the trade theory of comparative advantage: it collapses areas into points by assuming costless intra-areal transport and tends to regard the plant location process as one in which a pattern of location among multiple geographic points emerges on the basis of predetermined relative resource supplies and received prices at the points. The areal approach will often study a multi-region space-economy as a single area from which the plants seek to choose the best region for distance to raw materials[1] or markets.[2] The punctual approach will often assume that each region produces something of each good, whether or not the regional industry is optimally located with regard to the whole space-economy.[3] Whereas areal location theory considers degree of access to resources and distances to markets as susceptible to choice by the locating plant, punctual location theory takes resource supplies available to a regional industry as predetermined by their inelasticity and immobility and takes regional received prices as reflecting predetermined distances from the region to markets.

Both approaches to location theory are useful, but this chapter has forgone the advantages of the areal approach and used a punctual approach in order to take advantage of the trade-theoretic elements of H-O-J/W-T-M model of the previous chapter. By assuming constant returns to scale and no intermediate transport production, this essay has been able to interpret Jone's model of aspatial equilibrium as a model of an interregional pattern of production.

To reiterate, relations (24)-(30) are derived from a special case of the H-O-J/W-T-M industrial location model that imposes constant returns to scale, i.e., the elimination of agglomeration economies and of transport production as an intermediate user of scarce resources. This does not mean that the relations cannot be

[1]Emilio Casetti, "Optimal Location of Steel Mills Serving the Quebec and Southern Ontario Steel Market," Canadian Geographer 10 (1966) 27-39.

[2]Chauncy D. Harris, "The Market as a Factor in the Localization of Industry in the United States," Annals of the Association of American Geographers 17 (1954): 92-99.

[3]G. B. Norcliffe and J. H. Stevens, "The Heckscher-Ohlin Hypothesis and Structural Divergence in Quebec and Ontario, 1961-1969," Canadian Geographer 23 (1979): 239-54.

derived in some form without these restrictions, but only that they are less likely and that the whole process embodied in the activity analysis format of equations (2')-(5') and (18')-(21') becomes, in general, ambiguous without the restrictions. Kemp shows that the Rybczynski and Stolper-Samuelson versions of the relations may hold even under non-constant returns, but that a number of conditions, possibly severe, must also obtain.[1] This essay, instead, imposes constant returns in order to achieve the unambiguous theoretical results (26) and (30).

Yet, the assumptions about returns to scale and, implicitly, agglomeration and transport are not necessarily the most cumbersome restrictions imposed on the general H-O-J/W-T-M model to deduce the interregional version. The assumption of Jones's model[2] and relations (24)-(30) that each region produces only two commodities with only two factors seems a potentially far more difficult hypothesis to maintain in the face of all the multi-commodity, multi-factor regional economies that can be observed in the world. The next chapter undertakes to generalize the 2-by-2 results (26) and (30) for more complex regional economies.

---

[1] Kemp, Pure Theory, chap. 8.

[2] R. Jones, "General Equilibrium," p. 558.

CHAPTER V

GENERALIZING THE INTERREGIONAL MODEL FOR

MULTIPLE GOODS AND FACTORS

Although results (26) and (30) reveal the capacity for interregional analysis contained in the H-O-J/W-T-M location model, they
are based on the assumption that each region produces two goods with
two factors. Since the nonlinear programming version of the location
model in Chapter III permits an arbitrary number of goods and
factors,[1] it is well to discuss the generalization of the 2-by-2
case to higher dimensions. Jones points out that the basic change
effects in equations (24) and (28) result not from the dimension-
ality of the model but rather from an assumption of no joint production.[2] That is, several factors are assumed to be combined to
produce a single output, the technology of which is independent
of other products' technologies.[3] Under the assumption on non-
joint technology, therefore, it is reasonable to expect some version
of the 2-by-2 results (26) and (30) to obtain in higher dimensions.[4]

For an arbitrary but equal number of goods and factors (the
n-by-n case), the results are somewhat attenuated by the fact that
the effect of each endowment on each output or the effect of each
price on each wage cannot be unambiguously predicted. It is
possible, however, to establish the existence of associations between each endowment and some output and between each price and some
wage such that the powerful 2-by-2 results can be said to reflect
"essential properties" of the general n-by-n model[5] for regions

---

[1]See n. 4, p. 20 above.

[2]Ronald W. Jones, "Twoness" in Trade Theory: Costs and Benefits (Princeton,
N.J.: International Finance Section, Department of Economics, Princeton University,
1977).

[3]Henderson and Quandt, Microeconomic Theory, p. 79; Robert E. Hall, "The
Specification of Technology with Several Kinds of Output," Journal of Political
Economy 81 (1973): 878-92.

[4]Kemp (Three Topics, chap. 7) develops higher-dimensional versions of
results (26) and (30) that obtain under conditions of joint technology, provided
the number of factors is at least as great as the number of goods.

[5]Wilfred Ethier, "Some of the Theorems of International Trade with Many
Goods and Factors," Journal of International Economics 4 (1974): 199-206.

having a common technology. When the number of producible goods
exceeds the number of factors (the n > m case), it is still possible
to establish the existence of associations between some prices and
some wages which resemble the associations embodied in results (26)
and (30).[1]

Using Production Coefficients to Define
Factor Intensity with Multiple
Goods and Factors

Whereas the direction of the inequality signs in relations
(26) and (30) are predicted on the basis of the relative factor
intensities of the goods being compared, neither Ethier's nor Kemp's
generalization of the two-by-two equilibrium model offers a means
for deducing which goods are intensive in which factors. Indeed,
Vanek asserts that the factor endowments theory is not coherent
in a multi-factor, multi-good economy unless factor use is measured
as the total amount of a factor embedded in all goods produced by
the economy. Otherwise, the definition of factor intensity is ambiguous, since one good might be labor-intensive with respect to
another in terms of the labor-capital ratio but also capital-
intensive with respect to the capital-land ratio.[2]

Kemp, however, provides a way around some of the ambiguity
by presenting an algorithm for defining and identifying factor
intensities for an arbitrary number of factors and goods by comparing ratios of production coefficients. If

$$\frac{a_{ii}}{a_{ji}} > \frac{a_{is}}{a_{js}} \quad \begin{array}{l} \text{(for } i = 1, 2, \ldots, m; \\ s, j = 1, 2, \ldots, n; \\ s \neq i, \ j \neq i, \ n \geq m), \end{array}$$

then good i is intensive in the use of factor i (assuming there are
no factor intensity reversals for any equilibrium factor prices).[3]
Roughly speaking, a good is intensive in a factor if the ratio of
its production coefficients for the factor to coefficients of other
factors is greater than all other coefficient ratios of the good and
greater, too, than the corresponding ratios of other goods.

---

[1] Kemp, Three Topics, chap. 4.

[2] Jaroslav Vanek, "The Factor Proportions Theory: The N-Factor Case," Kyklos
21 (1968): 749-56.

[3] Kemp, Pure Theory, p. 48.

Kemp's principle can be illustrated with Lerner-Pearce diagrams. Figure 1 depicts a regional economy producing two goods with two factors under constant returns to scale. Factor endowments are fixed and output prices are given by national (or international) markets. The isoquants represent the quantities of each good that receive $1 of revenue in the region after fixed transport costs to market have been absorbed by the regional producers. At the given national prices and transport rates, it requires too much y_1 and y_2 to produce a dollar's worth of x_3 efficiently with the region's technology; so only x_1 and x_2 are produced. Chord AB is tangent to the $1 isoquants and forms a locus of convex combinations of the x_1 and x_2 quantities represented by the isoquants.

Assuming full employment of factor endowments, the optimal convex combination of goods produced by the region in figure 1 is determined by the intersection of the tangent chord AB with the factor endowment ratio line $(\bar{y}_1/\bar{y}_2)^R$, namely, point R*. In competitive equilibrium, the sum of payments for amounts y_{11}, y_{21}, y_{12}, y_{22} --used to produce the combination of x_1 and x_2 at R*--equals the $1 received for the composite output quantity at R*. The slope of AB is the (negative of the) factor wage ratio v_2/v_1, which itself is equal to the marginal rate of factor substitution in both x_1 and x_2. The factor proportions used to produce at R*, y_{11}/y_{21} and y_{12}/y_{22}, will exhaust the region's factor endowment.[1]

Technology determines the shape of the isoquants, and received prices determine the positions of the isoquants with respect to each other. The shapes and positions of the isoquants, in turn, determine the slope of the tangent chord and thereby the wages paid for the factor proportions used to produce at the point of tangency. As in relations (28)-(30), factor wages are determined by technology and prices. Relative factor endowments determine the slope of the endowment ratio line. In turn, this endowment line, for a tangent chord given by technology and prices, determines the intersection with the tangent and thereby the commodity composition of regional output. As in relations (24)-(26), for given prices, output proportions are determined by technology and factor endowments.

Rays OA and OB in figure 1 reflect y_{11}/y_{21} and y_{12}/y_{22}: the optimal ratios of factor amounts employed in producing $1 worth of x_1 and x_2. Since $y_{1j}/y_{2j} = (y_{1j}/x_j)/(y_{2j}/x_j) = a_{1j}/a_{2j}$, the factor

---

[1] See Harry G. Johnson, The Two-Sector Model of General Equilibrium (Chicago Aldine, 1971), chap. 1.

43

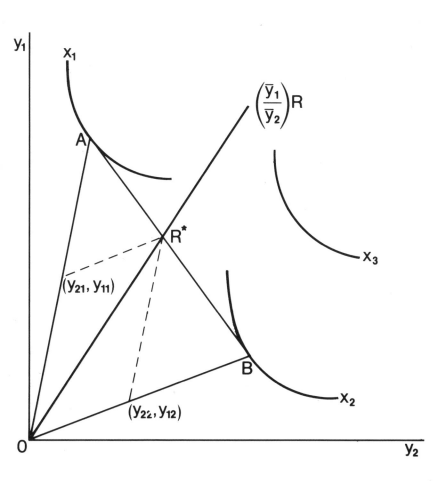

Fig. 1. A regional economy producing two goods with two factors

rays provide graphical representations of the production coefficient ratios needed for applying Kemp's principle in identifying factor-intensive goods.[1] For the regional equilibrium represented in chord AB, $a_{11}/a_{21} > a_{12}/a_{22}$; so x_1 is intensive in y_1.

Generalization of Price-Wage Result

Figure 2 illustrates how result (30) is reflected in cases where two regions are in equilibrium with two factors used to produce more than two goods. Since such an equilibrium implies, in general, that more than one output price differs across regions, the ceteris paribus assumption of result (30) is violated. Nevertheless, just as in that result, different received price ratios in figure 2 determine different regional wage ratios on the basis of factor intensity (assuming there are no factor intensity reversals between goods). Region 2 receives a higher price than region 1 for y_2-intensive x_2, and this causes a higher v_2/v_1 in region 2 than in region 1.

In the general case of n goods with m < n factors, relative wages of two of the m factors will change as in result (30), provided there is a change in the relative prices of two goods that can be associated with the factors by virtue of one good's using one factor more intensively than all other goods and the other good's using the other factor more intensively than all other goods. According to Kemp, these factor intensity relations can be identified by ratios of production coefficients.[2] In figure 2, for example, $a_{11}/a_{21} > a_{13}/a_{23} > a_{12}/a_{22}$ and $a_{22}/a_{12} > a_{23}/a_{13} > a_{21}/a_{11}$. By Kemp's principle, interregional differences in the relative prices of goods not having extreme factor intensities will not necessarily affect relative wages. For example, an interregional difference in the relative prices of x_1 and x_3 will not affect relative wages because the production points of the regions, R^1 and R^2 do not lie on the chord segments A^1C^1 and A^2C^2 which connect the x_1 and x_3 isoquants. The production points do, however, lie on the chord segment connecting the goods with the most extreme, and contrasting intensities: the prices of x_1 and x_2 determining the relative wages of y_1 and y_2.

Since two points determine a line, any other point on the line must be linearly dependent on the two points. This means that only

---

[1] Kemp, Pure Theory, chap. 1, Appendix.

[2] Ibid., pp. 33 and 48.

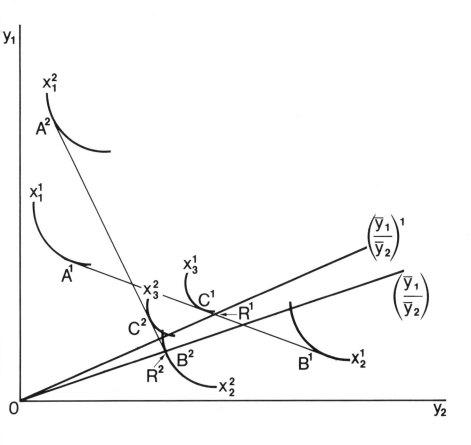

Fig. 2. Result (30) illustrated for two regions, each producing three goods with two factors

two of the prices implied by the $1 isoquants in figure 2 are neces-
sary to determine a tangent chord and (if the chord is intersected
by the regional endowment ray) relative wages. This is true of the
general case when it is observed that the equilibrium number n of
goods being produced exceeds the number of factors m: the over-
determinacy of the wages is resolved by the fact that unit costs of
n-m goods are dependent on the unit costs of the other m goods.[1]

Generalization of Endowment-Output Result

In contrast to result (30), result (26) theoretically cannot
be predicted for cases when the number of goods n exceeds the number
of factors m, even when factor intensities are identified. In the
price-wage result, the endogenous variables, i.e., wages, are the
smaller quantity in the n > m relation; but in the endowment-output
result, the endogenous variables, i.e., outputs, are the larger
quantity and therefore theoretically under-determined.[2]

> Within any [region] there is more than one configuration of [x_i's]
> that will maximize the value of [regional] product and also keep
> employment of all resources full at the well-determined factor prices.[3]

In geometric terms, the production transformation surface is ruled
whenever n > m; so the received price hyperplane can be tangent to
it along a straight line whereon an infinite number of different
convex combinations of outputs represent equally efficient equilibria.[4] The upshot is that, given technology and received prices,
regional factor endowment ratios influence rather than determine
regional output ratios.

An example of the theoretical indeterminacy of output proportions in the case of n = 4 > 2 = m is shown in figure 3. The
production combination of x_1 and x_2 in the amounts represented by
OS and OT, respectively, and the combination of x_3 and x_4 represented
by OW and OZ are equally efficient, competitive, and resource
exhausting. Nevertheless, the endowment ray $(\bar{y}_1/\bar{y}_2)^Q$ is steeper

---

[1] Samuelson, "Prices of Factors and Goods," pp. 8-9.

[2] G. Hadley, Linear Algebra (Reading, Mass.: Addison-Wesley, 1961),
pp. 167-73.

[3] Samuelson, "Prices of Factors and Goods," p. 9.

[4] James R. Melvin, "Production and Trade with Two Factors and Three Goods,"
American Economic Review 58 (December 1968): 1249-68.

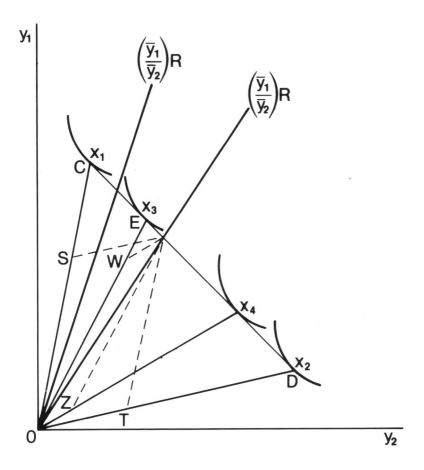

Fig. 3. The tendency toward result (26) illustrated for a
region producing four goods with two factors

than it is flat and intersects the equilibrium wage tangent CD at a point, Q, that makes OS > OT and OW > OZ. Inspection suggests that the y_1 endowment's being greater than the y_2 endowment creates a tendency for the y_1-intensive goods x_1 and x_3 to be produced in greater amounts than the y_2-intensive goods x_2 and x_4: a tendency similar to the endowment-output relation in result (26).

Kemp offers some rigorous theoretical support for the apparent tendency in figure 3, based on his algorithm for identifying factor-intensive goods with ratios of production coefficients. He proves that for the general case of n > m $\geq$ 2, a good must be produced by a region if: (1) its factor intensity (ratio of production coefficients) can be represented by an outer edge of an outer cone in a Lerner-Pearce diagram (e.g., ray OC in figure 3) and (2) the regional factor endowment ratio can be represented by a ray contained in an outer cone (e.g., cone COE).[1] In other words, when a good exhibits the highest intensity of all n goods in one of the m factors and there are no factor intensity reversals between goods, a region well-endowed with the intensive factor--i.e., such that the ratio of the factor's endowment to all other endowments is higher than all factor intensity ratios except for that of the intensive good--must produce the good. This principle recalls Jones's form of the Heckscher-Ohlin theory of the effect of physical factor abundance on output,[2] such as is embodied in result (26).

The necessity of producing a certain good follows from the assumptions that resource endowments are fully employed and that each good is produced with different factor proportions. If a region with endowment ray $(\bar{y}_1/\bar{y}_2)^R$ in figure 3 used its resources only in the production of x_2, x_3, and x_4, employing, say, 5 units of y_2 with 1 unit of y_1 for x_2, 3 units of y_2 with 2 of y_1 for x_4, and 2 units of y_2 with 3 of y_1 for x_3, without also using 1 unit of y_2 with 5 of y_1 for x_1, it would exhaust its given endowment of y_2 before using up all the endowment of y_1.[3] Since this structural

---

[1] Kemp, Pure Theory, p. 50. The rays and cones are defined for n factor proportion rays and one endowment ray in Euclidean m-space; so Kemp's principle does not depend on its being possible to graph the vectors in 2- or 3-space.

[2] R. Jones, "Factor Proportions." See also n. 3, p. 13 above.

[3] See Richard S. Eckaus, "The Factor Proportions Problem in Underdeveloped Areas," American Economic Review 45 (September 1955): 539-65.

redundancy of a factor is ruled out by the assumption of full employment,[1] x_1 must be produced in order to exhaust $\bar{y}_1$.

It is, moreover, reasonable to suspect that even when factor
intensities and endowments do not lie at the extremes posited in
Kemp's proof, the influence of factor abundance will be more likely
for intensities and endowments closer rather than farther from the
extreme. This is illustrated in figure 4. Full employment of the
factor amounts represented by OB, OD, and OE is possible; but in
that case there would be no production of x_1, the y_1-intensive good.
A more likely regional output combination would include at least
some quantity of x_1, perhaps such that the factor amounts of OA, OC,
OD, and OE. In this analysis, the fact that a good is intensive in
a factor makes it probable that the good will be produced by a region that possesses the factor; and, for any two commodities being
compared, the higher the relative endowment of a factor, the more
likely is the region to produce a higher proportion of the commodity
that is intensive in the abundant factor. Thus relative factor intensities and endowments should have effects on outputs in the multi-
commodity, multi-factor case similar to the effects in the two-
commodity, two-factor case of result (26).

Summary of the Generalized
Interregional Model

Kemp's criterion of high production coefficient ratios has
been used to infer which commodities and factors in a multi-
commodity, multi-factor economy will be associated as are the two
commodities and two factors in Jones's model.[2] Thus results (26)
and (30) of the 2-by-2 interregional model have been demonstrated to
reflect tendencies in regional economies with more goods than factors.
Interregional differences in received relative prices, with technology and endowments constant, determine interregional differences
in relative wages according to the relative factor intensities of
the goods. Interregional differences in relative factor endowments,

---

[1] Robert Dorfman, Paul A. Samuelson and Robert M. Solow, Linear Programming
and Economic Analysis (New York: McGraw-Hill, 1958), pp. 365-66, point out that
the possibility of full employment follows from the assumption of variable factor
proportions, which implies that any amount of one input can be combined with one
unit of another input without the marginal product of the intensive factor going
to zero. There can be no redundant factors as long as technology allows sub-
stituting one input for another indefinitely. In the case of the H-O-J/W-T-M
model, with its given prices and endowments, variable proportions means that the
Kuhn-Tucker proof of the existence of an optimal solution for outputs and wages
ipso facto guarantees the full employment of resource endowments.

[2] Kemp, Pure Theory, chap. 1, Appendix.; R. Jones, "General Equilibrium."

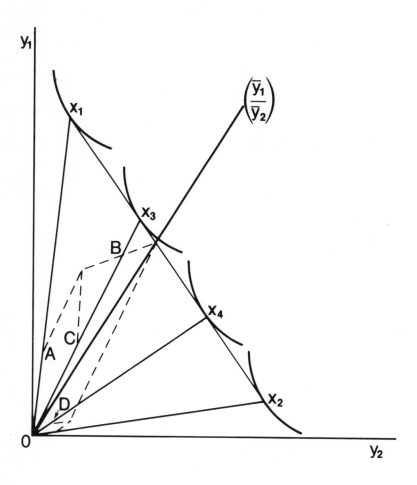

Fig. 4.   A region using two factors to produce either three or four goods

with technology and prices constant, create a presumption of inter-regional differences in output proportions based on the relative factor intensities of goods.

Although not as clear-cut as the 2-by-2 interpretations, the generalized interpretations of the results (26) and (30) are important because they provide a possible basis for empirically testing the interregional version of the H-O-J/W-T-M model with data from a multi-commodity, multi-factor economy. Commodities can be taken two at a time on the basis of contrasting factor intensities and then compared by using ratios of observed prices, outputs, wages, and endowments in the very formats in which results (26) and (30) are expressed. In this way, the general H-O-J/W-T-M model becomes an empirically testable theory of industrial geography.

CHAPTER VI

USING THE MODEL FOR

ECONOMIC GEOGRAPHIC RESEARCH

This chapter recapitulates the terms and implications of the industrial location model developed in previous chapters in order to suggest the general ways in which economic geographers might use the model. The essential elements of the model are discussed in respect to their implications for economic geographic research. These discussions are followed by a broad outline of the problems likely to be encountered in such research, along with some suggestions as to how the problems might be minimized.

Essential Elements of the Trade/Location Model

The general factor endowments/least-cost location model (H-O-J/W-T-M) comprises two main types of analysis: general equilibrium and cross-sectional. Understanding the basic assumptions of these types of analysis is essential to evaluating the model's usefulness to geographers. In addition, the interregional special case of the general model is designed to stress the general model's capabilities for cross-sectional analysis of regional production possibilities. The advantages of these capabilities to industrial location theorists derive from the fact that the trade-theoretic concept of comparative advantage can be seen as a concept of relative locational pull.

General Equilibrium Analysis in the Model

One of the model's main types of analysis assumes that the pattern of industrial location results from an economic process that tends towards general equilibrium. That is, plant location and output activities take place in the context of a multitude of interdependent supply and demand activities. The industrial geography of such an economic system cannot be fully comprehended unless account is taken of a plant's roles as both a demander of scarce resources such as labor and a supplier of commodities to competitive output markets.

The interdependent and competitive status of a locating plant means that its location and production decisions cause feedbacks that can alter the circumstances on which the decisions are based. For instance, locating in a region so as to use a certain cheap resource can drive up the wages of the resource, perhaps making the region less attractive to other prospective locaters. The location-decision process is interdependent with the resource supply and demand processes.

The most vivid example of the interdependence of site-selection with resource markets is in the least-cost (W-T-M) side of the general equilibrium model, where savings that result from nearness to resources or agglomeration benefits are shown to be susceptible to a compensating cost in higher site rent. Locations, like all other resources in the general equilibrium model, are scarce resources; so competition for their services must redound to the benefit of their owners (i.e., landlords). Furthermore, the H-O-J side of the model depicts how the scarcity of unique locations and the scarcity of resources used to produce transport services interact in such a way that regions produce their final goods under conditions of decreasing returns to scale. The higher the output level, the more are distant plant locations used, and, consequently, the more are resources required for the production of transport in addition to the production of final goods.

The interdependence and competition implied by the general equilibrium principle of the model encourage the economic geographer to look for economic checks and balances in the industrial location system. If one resource (e.g., labor) appears cheap in a region, look to see if another (e.g., site) is dear relative to other regions. If one region appears to offer absolutely low costs to producers, ask how long it might take before so many plants locate there that resource wages are driven up by competition.

The general equilibrium principle also implies that the industrial location and production process tends towards optimality, i.e., towards the state wherein any reallocation of resources would cause output value to decline in the sectors losing resources by more than output value would increase in the sectors gaining resources. General equilibrium analysis thus has normative implications for economic geographers who are interested in questions of policy. The efficiency costs and benefits of any single plant location or even a pattern of locations cannot be fully evaluated except in the context of the total allocation of resources in the space-economy. An allocation of resources to a region by, say, government redistribution or corporate monopoly fiat may permit the

receiving region to develop an optimal industrial mix with respect
to the constraints it faces after the allocation. At the same time,
the allocation may be sub-optimal with respect to the whole space-
economy because resources could be used more efficiently (produce
even greater output value) in other regions.

Even when optimal location policies are not at issue, the
optimality implication of general equilibrium can redirect the
attention of location theorists. This is because it is the assumption of optimality which permits the assumption of duality between
the least-cost location (W-T-M) and the factor endowments (H-O-J)
approaches to industrial location. The mathematical programming
concept of duality means that regions' minimizing their industrial
operating and location costs with respect to given output prices
can be achieved precisely by regions' maximizing the value of their
industrial output with respect to their given resource supplies.
This means that industrial geography is as much a matter of output
proportions and resource supplies as it is of costs and prices.
Location theorists, instead of devoting most of their attention
to costs and prices as locational determinants, might well devote
more attention to output levels and resource endowment quantities.

Cross-Sectional Analysis in the Model

Another main type of analysis comprised by the factor en-
dowments/least-cost location model assumes that the space-economy
is composed of technologically similar regions that can be compared
with each other cross-sectionally. Since all regions are assumed
to have access to the same technological knowledge, they can all
be regarded as cases of the same basic production structure.
Comparing two different regions over space is, therefore, like
comparing a single region at one point in time with itself at another
point in time. Regions are assumed to differ from each other
largely because of resource endowments, intraregional resource
transport distances, and distances to national (or international)
market points.

It is implicit in the cross-sectional principle that the
model allows a given industry to be represented in more than one
region, even in all regions. The assumption that world output
prices are not affected by the output of any region alone means
that a region need not be optimally located in order to produce a
good with positive income. As long as the world price is high
enough, suboptimally located regions can also produce (at higher
cost) with non-negative net income. Indeed, even the best-located

regions can take only limited advantage of the market because such
regions possess only limited supplies of resources with which to
produce the output. The cross-sectional principle of the model,
then, leads the economic geographer to look for the multiregional
patterns in an industry instead of one or several optimal regions
for the industry.

Using the model for cross-sectional analysis puts the em-
phasis of research on relative locational pull rather than absolute
locational pull. The main issue is not why an industry is pulled to
a region, for the model expects many industries to occur in all
regions. Instead, the main issue is why one industry is pulled
in a certain proportion to another industry or why two industries
are pulled to one region in a different proportion from their
proportion in another region. It is on this cross-sectional
principle that the model most clearly reveals its connection to
trade theory, for the study of relative locational pull is the
study of regional comparative advantage.

Interregional Comparison of
Production Possibilities

In order to concentrate on cross-sectional analysis, the
interregional special case of the general H-O-J/W-T-M model assumes
that intraregional transport is costless and the cost of transporting
output to markets is constant. This special case is designed for
the comparison of regions on the basis of differences in relative
resource endowments and relative output prices. Regions are compared to each other with ratios--rather than absolute levels--of
resource and production data. By examining relative quantities,
the interregional model can bring out interregional similarities
in industrial profiles that are obscured by concentrating only
on absolute quantities. For example, a region with large absolute
resource endowments and a region with small absolute endowments
may have endowment ratios of similar sizes and therefore might be
expected to pull given industries in similar proportions.

The factor endowments side of the interregional model has
output proportions determined by input endowment proportions, and
the least-cost location side of the model has regional relative
wages determined by relative received prices, which are themselves
determined by world prices and distances from regions to markets.
Resource amounts and market distances thereby delimit each region's
production possibilities; so the model induces the economic geographer
to see the pattern of comparative advantage or relative locational
pull as a pattern of production possibilities.

Since cross-sectional analysis assumes that all regions have
the same production structure (technology) but different production
possibilities (resources and received prices), the model virtually
defines regions by their production possibilities. As in Rawstron's
scheme, plants are not expected to locate at a single best site,
but rather to locate in any regions where production is viable
without incurring negative income.[1] What prevents all plants being
pulled only to the region offering the absolutely lowest cost are
the limitations imposed by finite resources combined with fixed
output prices. Any output amounts greater than the full-employment
equilibrium amounts implied by the region's production possibilities
will drive the wages of inelastically supplied resources up such
that factor payments exceed given prices and some plants must cut
back production to avoid negative income. That a given industry
occurs in some regions but not in others is caused largely by the
fact that supply and demand conditions limit or even preclude the
viability of some regions as plant locations for the industry.

The H-O-J/W-T-M model regards the space-economy as being
composed of geographic units with borders that are spatial margins
past which it is assumed that no resources may be moved and at
which it is assumed that the received prices of outputs change due
to changes in the transport costs to output markets. Chisholm and
Smith also employ the concept of a spatial margin to delimit areas
of production possibilities. For these writers, however, the
spatial margin is an isoline at which cost just equals revenue and
beyond which cost exceeds revenue and production becomes uneconomi-
cal.[2] This is a case of areal location theory in that the Chisholm
and Smith models are designed to determine the margin of production,
i.e., to define the region according to the increasing cost of
transport as a function of distance from some geographic center.
In contrast, the cross-sectional analysis of the H-O-J/W-T-M model,
especially in its interregional version, takes the margins of
production as already given by politics (e.g., state boundaries)
or historical development (e.g., the economic integration of the
Chicago-Gary areas) or even statistical expediency (e.g., Census
divisions). In its cross-sectional aspect, the model is a case of
punctual location theory. It is designed to determine the industrial
profile of predetermined regions having production possibilities that

---

[1]Rawstron, "Three Principles."

[2]Michael Chisholm, Geography and Economics (New York: Praeger, 1966);
Smith, Industrial Location.

are predetermined by the resources available and the output prices
received within the boundaries defined by politics, economic history,
or accessibile sets of geographical data.

Just as the model differentiates regions by their production
possibilities, it differentiates industries by their production
requirements or input requirements. As does Rawstron, the model
analyzes these requirements not as a lump figure but rather as
a set of individual input components. In this way, it treats
production requirements as relative requirements. Though many industries use the same kind of productive factors, they use them in
different proportions, i.e., different factor intensities. Regions
with different production possibilities--relative resource endowments and relative received prices--have different comparative advantages because their endowment and price ratios accord with
different combinations of factor intensity ratios, i.e., with
different combinations of industries. The interregional model re-
lates industrial location patterns to a "physical" congruency between production (factor) proportions and regional (resource and
price) proportions. In using the model, the economic geographer
looks for a meshing of industrial requirements with regional possibilities.

Problems in Using the Model for Research

The general H-O-J/W-T-M model, including its interregional
special case, is not applicable to all space-economies; and the
economic geographer must remain mindful of the type of economic
system implied by the essential elements of the model. In particular,
the general equilibrium principle may be violated by unemployed
resources and decidedly will be violated by inefficiently allocated
production. These suboptimal circumstances may imply less than
complete interdependence of markets or less than perfect competition
within markets. One way the geographer might minimize the likelihood
of such conditions is by applying the model to space-economies that
are subject to "relatively" little government intervention and that
comprise "relatively" few persons or firms with great market (mono-
polistic) power.

Similarly, the cross-sectional principle will be violated
if the regions being compared do not have a common production
structure, i.e., if the regions have access to different levels
of technology. The economic geographer might minimize the likelihood of regional technological differences by applying the model
to interregional systems that have well-developed communications

and present few obstacles to the implementation of efficient inno-
vations.

Even if the geographer can decide whether a space-economy
has relatively free competition and efficient flows of ideas, the
interregional special case of the model may have difficulty in
revealing regional comparative advantage. This is because the
model derives comparative advantage from production possibilities,
and it is likely that those space-economies that are most amenable
to general equilibrium conditions and cross-sectional analysis are
also space-economies that afford the widest variety of production
possibilities to their regions. The economy may be so integrated
and efficient that resources are (1) highly mobile between regions
or (2) rapidly reproducible in response to industrial demand. Then
the location of an industry in a region attracts new resources and
the direction of causation is obscured in the endowment-output
hypothesis of the model. Few resources are completely immobile; but,
since minerals are generally non-reproducible, farm land requires
soil conditions, and timber stands take time to grow, the economic
geographer might circumvent the question of elastic or inelastic
regional factor supplies when studying land-derived resources and
resource-based industries.

Whether or not the regions' resources are basically immobile
and inelastically supplied, an economy that is amenable to general
equilibrium and cross-sectional analysis may have technology so
flexible that any region can manipulate it to produce a great
number of different goods efficiently. In this situation of multiple
goods and factors, the interregional model implies that the relationships among output and endowment proportions and price and wage
ratios are not perfectly determinate. Even when output proportions
and relative wages do reflect endowment proportions and relative
prices according to the factor intensity ratios of the various goods,
the large number of goods--and, consequently, ratios--may still make
the observable differences among regional ratios so small as to
elude empirical analysis. Apropos of the uncertainties and ambigu-
ities in cases of multiple goods and factors, the model predicts
that the economic geographer will observe the endowment-output and
price-wage relationships most clearly when the goods under study
exhibit maximally contrasting factor intensity ratios.

Summary of the Model in Research

The general trade/location model (H-O-J/W-T-M) is designed
to analyze the industrial geography of an economy that is amenable
to general equilibrium and cross-sectional analysis. That is, the

model assumes the space-economy is characterized by a high degree
of market interdependence and competition and is composed of regions
sharing a common store of technological knowledge. The interregional special case of the model stresses the congruence between
production requirements and production possibilities, i.e., between
industries' factor intensity ratios and regions' resource endowment
and relative price ratios.

The most serious problems in using such a model to study
patterns of industrial location derive from the likelihood that
space-economies with high degrees of interdependence and competition
and with technologically similar regions will also be space-economies
that exhibit a complex variety of regional production possibilities.
One way the economic geographer can contend with the empirical
complications due to elasticity and mobility of resource supplies
or multiplicity of output types is to apply the interregional model
to cases where the essential structure it predicts has the best
chance of "showing through." An example is the case of regional
industries that exhibit contrasting intensities in the use of
natural or land-derived resources. This example is illustrated in
the following chapter.

CHAPTER VII

THE MODEL'S USE ILLUSTRATED:

EMPIRICAL TESTING OF THE

ENDOWMENT-OUTPUT RESULT

This chapter presents empirical tests of result (26) in chapter
IV for various pairs of commodities in the multi-factor, multi-
commodity United States economy.

$$\frac{\bar{y}_1^1}{\bar{y}_2^1} > \frac{\bar{y}_1^2}{\bar{y}_2^2} \div \frac{x_1^1}{x_2^1} > \frac{x_1^2}{x_2^2} \ , \tag{26}$$

where $\bar{y}_i^k$ is the endowment of resource i in region k and x_j^k is the
output of good j by region k.

The general purpose of empirically testing this endowment-
output formula is to determine whether and to what extent the theory
developed in the H-O-J/W-T-M model in chapters II-V can be made to
yield concrete implications for the real world. This will illustrate
the usefulness of the model for geographic research. One concrete
implication of the model's interregional special case is that
regional resource endowment proportions influence the commodity
composition of regional output in the direction predicted by the
factor proportions hypothesis of Heckscher-Ohlin trade theory.
Thus a specific purpose of testing result (26) is to measure the
applicability of trade theory to the geographic pattern of production
in the United States.[1]

The present tests are cross-sectional analyses of the United
States space-economy for given years. As was discussed in chapter
IV, the trade-theoretic location model, i.e., the interregional
case of the general H-O-J/W-T-M model, takes a punctual approach

---

[1]The testing of result (30), the dual of result (26) in chapter IV, is
not undertaken because of a severe lack of data. Regionally differentiated wages
are sometimes available for some factors (e.g., labor wages, mineral prices), but
regionalized prices of final goods seem extremely scarce. Those regional prices
that are available are usually in the form of a composite level index. Absolute
prices of individual goods are usually given only for the nation as a whole. By
the terms of the interregional model, such prices would have to be discounted
for each region according to some measure of each region's transport costs to
nationally determined markets. That daunting task is eschewed in this paper.

to location theory by studying industrial location as a property of
the economic relationships among regions. In contrast, the areal
approach to location theory studies location primarily as a function
of distances within a region. Many areal studies concentrate on
the locational pattern of a single industry--largely as a function of
transport costs--within a single area (region, country, province).[1]
The tests presented here, however, are interregional: they study the
patterns in which multiple industries are located as pairs or groups
in regions. As in trade theory, regions are collapsed into points
in the sense that movement within them is assumed costless. The
particular regions studied are chosen such that their resources can
plausibly be assumed interregionally immobile or at least far from
perfectly mobile. The subject of the tests, therefore, is not an
individual regional industry but rather the relationship among all
regions as reflected in the different proportions in which different
industries are represented in different regions.

Specifically, the tests compare the output proportions of regions' industries with the endowment proportions of regions' resources
in a format like that of result (26). The tests consist of estimating
the correlation between the ratios

$$\left(\frac{\text{Output of Industry 1}}{\text{Output of Industry 2}}\right) \text{ and } \left(\frac{\text{Endowment of Resource 1}}{\text{Endowment of Resource 2}}\right)$$

to see if the sign of the correlation coefficient is predicted by the
relative resource-intensities of the two industries.

Assumptions of the Tests

A proper test of the interregional model developed in chapters
IV and V must assume that all regions share the same technological
knowledge, that resource supplies are exogenous, i.e., limited and
separated by region, that each region takes output prices as given
by national (or international) markets, and that the goods being
compared exhibit highly contrasting intensities in the use of
different factors.[2] The assumption that all regions have access

---

[1]See, e.g., Olaf Lindberg, "An Economic Geographical Study of the Localization of the Swedish Paper Industry," Geografiska Annaler 35 (1953): 28-40;
Casetti, "Optimal Location of Steel Mills."

[2]The interregional model makes two other notable assumptions: constant
returns to scale technology and no factor intensity reversals (see chapter IV).
Although there is evidence of non-constant returns in regional production functions
(see Paul S. Land, "The Interregional Comparison of Production Functions,"
Regional Science and Urban Economics 8 [1978]: 339-53), it is a maintained
hypothesis of the empirical tests that regionally aggregated industrial production
functions are close enough to being homogeneous degree one that the endowment-
output result will "show through." Factor intensity reversals are unlikely in
the present tests because the goods are selected for low elasticities of

to the same technology is not unreasonable in the highly sophisticated
and integrated United States space-economy. Cross-sectional testing
is then a matter of spatial comparative statics: comparing two
technologically similar regions is equivalent to comparing one
region at a point in time with itself at another point in time.

For the purpose of ensuring as much exogeneity as possible
for the factor endowments, the tests study regional endowments
of natural or land-derived resources and take regions to be the
nine groupings of contiguous states defined as Geographic Divisions
by the Census of Manufactures [1]:

> New England: Maine, Vermont, New Hampshire, Massachusetts, Connecticut,
> Rhode Island;
> Middle Atlantic: New York, Pennsylvania, New Jersey;
> East North Central: Wisconsin, Michigan, Illinois, Indiana, Ohio;
> West North Central: North Dakota, South Dakota, Minnesota, Nebraska, Iowa,
> Kansas, Missouri;
> South Atlantic: West Virginia, Maryland, Delaware, Virginia, North Carolina,
> South Carolina, Georgia, Florida;
> East South Central: Kentucky, Tennessee, Alabama, Mississippi;
> West South Central: Oklahoma, Arkansas, Texas, Louisiana;
> Mountain: Idaho, Montana, Wyoming, Nevada, Utah, Colorado, Arizona, New
> Mexico;
> Pacific: Washington, Oregon, California.

Water supplies are heavily dependent on climate, agriculture
requires soil conditions, timber stands take years to grow, and
mineral deposits are usually not replenished; so natural resource
supplies can be regarded as largely inelastic. Defining regions
as groups of states takes account of the likelihood that raw
materials will often be transported from their original sources in
one state to production locations in another state. Although raw
materials from one Census division may sometimes be transported to
another division, it is assumed that enough of the natural resources
are consumed within their division of origin that they can be
considered interregionally immobile. With a few exceptions, such
as putting eastern Ohio, western Pennsylvania, and northern West
Virginia in three different divisions, the Census regionalization
of American industry is reasonable as a first approximation. A
maintained hypothesis of the tests is that regional industries
produce a large enough proportion of their output from indigenous
resources that the fundamental ratio relationships predicted by
result (26) will "show through" empirically.

---

substitution between the two inputs tested: they use one resource in very large
amounts relative to their use of the other resource.

[1] See, e.g., U.S. Bureau of the Census, Census of Manufactures: 1958,
vol. 3, Area Statistics (Washington, D.C.: Government Printing Office, 1961),
p. viii.

In assuming that a region takes output prices as given, the H-O-J-/W-T-M (and interregional) model assumes that the region must consume its products at nationally determined prices and can export any amounts of these products without affecting the given prices. The region's output proportions are therefore assumed to be independent of local demand,[1] and output data rather than trade flow data are used to test the Heckscher-Ohlin theory of factor endowments. The upshot is that trade theory is allowed to work as location theory without the burden of explaining why a region consumes or exports its output in a certain proportion.

In a multi-factor, multi-good regional economy, the interregional model predicts that the endowment-output result is most likely to be observed when the goods being compared are highly intensive in different factors. By Kemp's principle,[2] it is not enough that a good is more intensive than all the other tested goods in a particular factor. In addition, the factor must constitute a larger proportion than all the other tested factors of the total[3] input requirements of the good. For example, the ratio of highly timber-intensive sawmill products to highly petroleum-intensive oil products is compared to the ratio of forest land to petroleum reserves.

Design and Justification of the Tests

A number of other authors have used regional output data to test the factor endowments hypothesis for North American space-economies. Unlike the test presented here, however, the previous studies rely more on intraregional than interregional comparisons. They decide on some basis that a region is relatively well endowed with a factor and then compare factor intensity ratios of industries

---

[1] The assumption of demand-independence is arguably harder to sustain with regard to international--as opposed to interregional--trade and production (see Stephan Valavanis-Vail, "Leontief's Scarce Factor Paradox," Journal of Political Economy 52 [1954]: 523-28) and this may account for some of the instances when trade flow data have failed to support the Heckscher-Ohlin hypothesis as a trade theory (e.g., Wassily Leontief, "Domestic Production and Foreign Trade: The American Capital Position Reexamined," Economia Internazionale 7 [1954]: 9-45; Wassily Leontief, "Factor Proportions and the Structure of American Trade," Review of Economics and Statistics 13 [1956]: 386-407; Robert E. Baldwin, "Determinants of the Commodity Structure of U.S. Trade," American Economic Review 61 [1971]: 126-46).

[2] Kemp, Pure Theory, chap. 1, Appendix. See chapter V above.

[3] Since the interregional model assumes constant returns (see n. 2, p. 57 above), unit and total input proportions are assumed to be the same.

with some measure of the percentage of national value added by each industry within the region (concentration ratios or location quotients[1]). The endowment-output hypothesis is supported if the industries most intensive in the region's relatively plentiful resource are also the industries with the highest concentration ratios or location quotients.[2]

Yet comparing production levels within regions is not the most appropriate test of the factor endowments theory, which is, after all, a theory of relative production proportions among regions. Strictly speaking, it would be possible for two regions to have the same concentration ratios or location quotients for one good but still to produce the good in differing proportions to another good.[3] The output proportions are significant data which, by the theory underlying the H-O-J/W-T-M model, reflect regional comparative advantage. Suppose, for instance, that good 1 is intensive in the use of factor 1. Regions A and B might both produce more of good 1 than good 2 because both regions are endowed with more of factor 1 than factor 2. Nevertheless, region A might still have a comparative advantage in good 1 because its endowment ratio of factor 1 to factor 2 is higher. The intraregional comparison of concentration ratios or location quotients does not necessarily discriminate between two such regions. The present tests, on the other hand, compare production ratios with endowment ratios to see whether the production ratios are accurately predicted by the comparative advantage implied in the endowment ratios.

---

[1] A concentration ratio of a regional industry is the value added by the industry in the region divided by the value added by the industry nationally. Thomas A. Klaasen, "Regional Comparative Advantage in the United States," Journal of Regional Science 13 (1973): 97-105. A location quotient is regional per capita value added divided by national per capita value added. John R. Moroney and James M. Walker, "A Regional Test of the Heckscher-Ohlin Hypothesis," Journal of Political Economy 74 (1966): 573-86.

[2] Moroney and Walker, "A Regional Test"; Edwin F. Estle, "A More Conclusive Test of the Heckscher-Ohlin Hypothesis," Journal of Political Economy 75 (1967): 886-88; John R. Moroney, The Structure of Production in American Manufacturing (Chapel Hill: University of North Carolina Press, 1972); Klaasen, "Regional Comparative Advantage"; John R. Moroney, "Natural Resource Endowments and Comparative Costs: A Hybrid Model of Comparative Advantage," Journal of Regional Science 15 (1975): 139-50; Norcliffe and Stevens, "Heckscher-Ohlin Hypothesis."

[3] For example, suppose x_j^k is the amount of good j produced in region k. The fact that two concentration ratios are equal, $x_1^1/x_1^{US} = x_1^2/x_1^{US}$, obviously does not contain enough information to determine whether $x_1^1/x_2^1 = x_1^2/x_2^2$.

Figure 5 uses the ratio approach to illustrate the different
regional industrial profiles in a two-good economy. At the nationally determined relative price $\bar{P}_1/\bar{P}_2$, region A is able to produce
relatively more of good 1 than is region B. This does not mean A
necessarily can produce absolutely more x_1 than can B (i.e., that
A's concentration ratio is higher than B's) but only that A can
produce x_1 in greater proportion to x_2. By Jones's version of
the Heckscher-Ohlin factor abundance theory, this comparative
advantage is due to region A's possessing relatively more of factor
1, in which x_1 is intensive.[1] Region A's comparative advantage
is illustrated in figure 6 (from which figure 5 could be derived).
At point Q*, for instance, region A can increase production of
x_1 at a lower opportunity cost of having to decrease production of
x_2.

Statistical Procedure

With nine regions (Census Geographical Divisions), thirty-six
unique interregional comparisons are possible for each pairing of
endowment and output ratios. In order to obtain a manageable number
of comparisons, endowment and output ratios of each region, as
formulated in result (26), are put in order of their rank among
all regions. The correlations between the ranks of the endowment
and output ratios are then measured in order to see whether or not
the estimated values are similar to the correlations predicted
by result (26) for a multi-factor, multi-good economy on the
basis of the contrasting factor intensities of the goods under
study.

For example, if industry 1 is intensive in the use of lumber
and industry 2 in petroleum, then result (26) predicts: the national
rank of a region's ratio ($\frac{\text{Output of Industry 1}}{\text{Output of Industry 2}}$) will be positively
correlated with the national rank of the region's ratio
($\frac{\text{Endowment of Forest}}{\text{Endowment of Petroleum}}$).

Since the interregional model only predicts that the endowment-
output result is likely to be observed for goods with contrasting
factor intensities, the use of only two factors to explain an output
ratio involves a theoretical risk of biased results due to the
omission of other important determinants.[2] The present tests seek to

---

[1] R. Jones, "Factor Proportions." See chapter II above.

[2] Jon Harkness and John F. Kyle, "Factors influencing United States
Comparative Advantage," Journal of International Economics 5 (1975): 153-65,
incorporate multiple productive factors (and other independent variables) into
a test of the Heckscher-Ohlin factor endowments hypothesis as a trade theory.

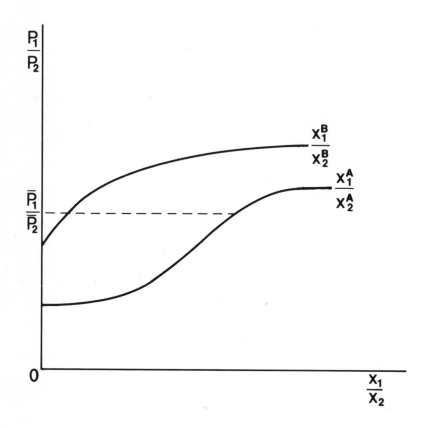

Fig. 5. A two-good economy in which region A has a comparative advantage in the production of x_1

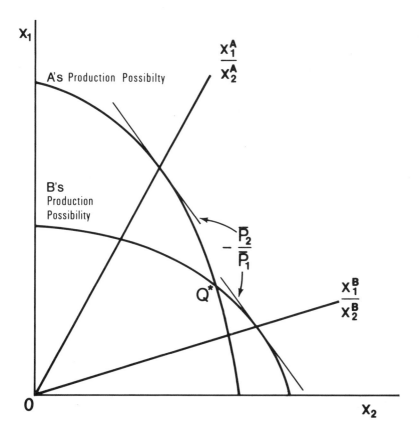

Fig. 6. The regions have different production possibility
curves because region A is relatively abundantly endowed with
factor 1, used intensively in producing x_1

limit the risk by avoiding altogether a parametric specification
of the relation between output and endowment ratios. No attempt
is made to predict the size of the output ratio from the size of
the endowment ratio. Instead, ranks of output ratios are predicted
from ranks of endowment ratios, with the calculated rank correlation
estimating the degree to which the predictions are accurate.

The rank correlation statistic that is calculated in the
tests is Spearman's r:

$$r = 1 - \frac{6}{N^3 - N} \sum_{k=1}^{N} [\text{rank}(x_1^k/x_2^k) - \text{rank}(\bar{y}_1^k/\bar{y}_2^k)]^2 ,$$

where N is the number of regions observed. Each two-resource
ratio (e.g., $\bar{y}_1/\bar{y}_2$) is assumed to have a probability distribution,
with the probability of a particular ratio value related to the
geophysical conditions under which a region is likely to possess
such resource proportions. Each two-industry ratio (e.g., x_1/x_2)
is assumed to have a probability distribution, with the probability
of a particular ratio value related to the historical and economic
conditions (including resource ratios) under which a region is
likely to produce such output proportions.

The ratios of actually existing regions do not constitute
the whole populations addressed by the statistical procedure. If
there existed other technologically similar regions in the United
States space-economy with other geophysical conditions and economic
histories, then there would exist other endowment and output ratios
having probable sizes in accordance with the same probability
distributions as the existing ratios. So it is that the objective
of the tests is broader than merely determining the correlations
among observed ratios. The objective is estimating a general
property ascribed by the interregional model to endowment-output
relations, namely, the correlations of whole populations of possible
ratios, both existing and hypothetical. The ratios of existing
regions therefore constitute a sample drawn, in a sense, by nature
and economic history.

Neither the relation between endowment ratio and geophysics
nor the relation between output ratio and economic history is
specified in the test; but, since the regions are assumed to be
too small to affect national demand and to have separate, unshared
resource supplies, an output or endowment ratio of a certain size
in one region does not imply, or does not induce, a corresponding
ratio of any particular size in any other region. That is, the
possible output and endowment ratios are independent random variable
so the observed ratios constitute random samples. Under these

circumstances, values of r may be ascribed significance levels
by using r to test the null hypothesis of no correlation between
the ranks of output ratios and ranks of endowment ratios.[1]
The statistical methodology employed in the tests is more
commensurate with the format of result (26) than with the format
of equations (24) in chapter IV: it predicts only that a region's
output ratio will be greater than another's as its endowment ratio
is greater, rather than predicting the actual size of the difference.
Correlations between ranks are measured with non-parametric
estimators; so that even the functional relationship among ranks
is not specified. The statistical procedure of the tests thus
embodies the minimal, but essential, point of the endowment-output
result.

Factor intensities of goods are difficult to specify exactly
in the case of raw materials. The Census of Manufactures carries
data on water usage by industry and the "Transactions Table of the
Input Output Study" carries data on amounts paid to broadly defined
raw materials producers for all output (resource products but also
other goods and services).[2] These sources are generally sufficient
for detecting an industry that is indisputably a large user of
a certain resource (e.g., the wood products industry's use of
forest resources).

Result (26) assumes the received output prices are held
constant when comparing regional endowments and output combinations.
By the W-T-M portion of the location model and its interregional
result (30), different relative prices induce different relative
wages, which with technologies that permit factor substitution,
induce different factor proportions in production. Since the factor
rays in figures 1 through 4 are constructed according to the optimal
factor proportions denoted by the wage lines' tangencies to the $1
isoquants, different prices and wages among regions will imply
different factor cones. The same endowment ray could therefore
exert less of an influence on the production of a given good in
one region than in another. Since the tests are based on non-
parametric functions of rankings, rather than direct specifications

---

[1]Alexander M. Mood, Franklin A. Graybill and Duane C. Boes, Introduction
to the Theory of Statistics, 3rd ed. (New York: McGraw-Hill, 1974), p. 526.

[2]See, e.g., U.S. Bureau of the Census, Census of Manufactures: 1958,
vol. 1, Summary Statistics (Washington, D.C.: Government Printing Office, 1961),
sect. 11 and Survey of Current Business 45 (September 1965): 33-49.

of endowment-output relations, this possible violation of the
ceteris paribus assumption of result (26) can only be serious if
interregional price differences are very large.[1]

Data

Natural Resource Endowments

Although statistics on average runoff are used to indicate
regional water resources, on forest land area to indicate timber
resources, and on petroleum reserves to indicate petroleum resources,
measures of the actual physical resource endowments of a region are
not otherwise used in the ratio tests. This is because such
measures are difficult or impossible to obtain; and even when
obtained, they are often inadequate.

One reason it is hard to measure natural resource endowments
is the dearth of knowledge about subsurface mineral deposits. This
is reflected in the fact that standardized reports on the size of
deposits are rare or nonexistent. The Minerals Yearbook, for
instance, rarely publishes geographically complete estimates of
reserve sizes for any non-fuel minerals except, occasionally, iron
ore. In many cases, when reserve estimates are published, they
are qualified as "inferred" rather than proven.[2]

Even when accurate knowledge of subsurface geology is available,
the significance of the endowments for the location of production
depends to a large extent on the current states of extraction
technology and mineral supply and demand. McDivitt and Manners
point out how the purely physical definition of mineral endowment
is open-ended: technically, most minerals demand could be met by
extracting the tiny deposits found in common rocks. The processing
of a large enough quantity of rocks would be too costly at con-
temporary prices, but the point remains that defining a region's
minerals endowment in purely physical terms may not define its
production possibilities.[3]

Deposits of Lake Superior iron ore were a major influence on
the location of the American steel industry. As these deposits

---

[1]However large the interregional price difference equations (24) in
chapter IV show that the effect on output differences depends on σ, the elasticity
of transformation, which is bound to be small when the goods have been selected
for having low elasticities of substitution (see R. Jones, "General Equilibrium,"
p. 563) between the raw material inputs.

[2]James F. McDivitt and Gerald Manners, Minerals and Men, rev.`ed.
(Baltimore: Johns Hopkins Press, 1974), p. 75.

[3]Ibid., pp. 11ff.

approached "exhaustion," the steel production possibilities of the
North Central region seemed to be diminishing. Technology, however,
redefined those possibilities by making the previously unexploitable
taconite ore an economically feasible raw material.[1] Taconite
pelletizing thereby effectively altered the resource endowment of
the Great Lakes.

Vanek and Moroney circumvent the problems of ambiguity and
lack of information in natural resource evaluation by considering
the products of primary natural resource industries rather than
natural resources per se.[2] The following ratio tests are likewise
based on the argument that the output of industries which process
natural resources as raw inputs--e.g., the agriculture, fishing,
logging, or mining industries--are the generally most meaningful
index of a region's technologically and economically usable resource
endowment. A region could not, in general, process the resources
unless it were endowed with the resources in the first place. The
maintained hypothesis will be that the proportions of resources
processed by one region relative to another reflect the proportions
possessed by one region relative to another.[3]

The endowments (processing industry outputs) are expressed in
terms of value in dollars rather than in terms of tonnages. This
facilitates aggregating different individual resources or grades
of the same resource into a composite resource: e.g., copper, lead,
and zinc values into base metal value or softwood and hardwood
values into forest resource value. The likelihood of anomalous
data is reduced by using an average of the region's resource product
value for several selected years: e.g., 1910, 1930, and 1950.
Here, the use of dollars as units of measure requires deflating
the value data by a wholesale price index in order to obtain uniform
historical averages expressed in constant real dollars.

---

[1] Ibid., pp. 42-47.

[2] Jaroslav Vanek, "The Natural Resource Content of Foreign Trade, 1870-1955,
and the Relative Abundnace of Natural Resource in the United States," Review of
Economics and Statistics 41 (1959): 146-53; Moroney, "Natural Resource Endowments."

[3] In Heckscher's ("Effect of Trade"), Ohlin's (Trade), and R. Jones's ("General Equilibrium") formulations of the endowment-output result, the endowments are
assumed to be exogenous variables, whereas it could be argued that the outputs
of primary resource processing industries are not exogenous but rather endogenous
to the general level of economic activity in the region. This objection is
largely overcome if it can be assumed that the portion of resource processing
due to the level of economic activity is proportional to the total amount of
resource processing and that the coefficient of proportionality is the same for
all resources in the region that are studied. This is equivalent to assuming,
say, that the output of both Pacific petroleum and Pacific timber in 1958 are due
in the same proportion to the level of growth in the Pacific economy; so that the

Regional Industrial Output

The tests endeavor to approximate the H-O-J/W-T-M model's assumption of given world prices by defining industries at highly aggregated levels: two and three-digit standard Industrial Classification (SIC) codes. It is reasonable to assume that competitive markets exist in broadly defined industries such as chemicals and steel.

There is little consistent data available on physical output quantities; so, like most previous regional tests of the endowment-output hypothesis,[1] the present tests are constrained to use value added as the measure of an industry's output. This requires assuming a reasonable degree of proportionality between value added and physical amounts produced. Using dollar amounts does, however, assist in industry aggregation by providing a common unit of measurement for the different goods included under the rubric of a single two-digit SIC code.[2]

Test Results

Table 1 gives the presumed intensities of the industries under study. In all cases, the correlations are predicted by the model to be positive on the basis of the factor intensities of the goods involved. That is, the industry in the numerator of the output ratio is presumed to be relatively intensive in its use of the resource in the numerator of the endowment ratio.

The computed endowment ratios are listed and ranked in appendix A, and the computed output ratios are listed and ranked in appendix B.[3] The Spearman rank correlation coefficients (r) of selected

---

coefficients of proportionality cancel out when petroleum and timber endowments (processing) are put in a ratio.

[1] See n. 2, p. 60, above.

[2] Strictly speaking, the Census of Manufactures for value added are not completely comparable among regions because they are in nominal terms, i.e., they are in terms of received regional prices, exclusive of freight costs: see, e.g., U.S. Bureau of the Census, Census of Manufactures: 1958, vol.1. Summary Statistics (Washington, D.C.: Government Printing Office, 1961), pp. 11-13 for definitions of "Value of Shipment" and "Value Added." This is, in fact, the way prices are supposed to vary interregionally according to the assumption of the H-O-J/W-T-M model: due to regionally varying costs of transporting output to national markets. Using "Value Added" for cross-sectional comparisons might thus be said to require a deflation for each region that reflects transport costs to market For the same reasons of expediencey that precluded testing the price-wage result (30) (see n. 1, p. 56), such deflations are not attempted in the present tests.

[3] The change in the absolute size of a given ratio of values added from one Census year to another can be due to a change in the relative prices of the goods in the ratio. This will not affect the accuracy of the endowment-output hypothesi if prices change in the same proportion in all regions.

TABLE 1

RESOURCE INTENSITIES OF TESTED INDUSTRIES BY STANDARD
INDUSTRIAL CLASSIFICATION (SIC) CODE

SIC Code	Industry	Intensive Resources
20	Food and kindred products	Extracted agricultural & fishery resources
21	Tobacco manufactures	Extracted agricultural resources
22	Textile mill products	Extracted agricultural resources
24	Lumber and products, except furniture	Extracted forest resources
26	Paper and allied products	Water, extracted forest resources
28	Chemicals and allied products	Extracted minerals
29	Petroleum and coal products	Crude petroleum, extracted minerals
31	Leather and leather products	Extracted agricultural resources
32	Stone, clay, and glass products	Non-metallic ores: clay, gypsum, sand & gravel, stone; extracted minerals
33	Primary metal industries	Coal, iron ore, base metal ores: copper, lead, zinc; extracted minerals
331, 332	Iron and steel industry	Coal, iron ore
333, 334, 335, 336	Nonferrous metal industries	Base metal ores: copper, lead, zinc

Note: According to U.S. Bureau of the Census, Census of Manufactures: 1958, vol. 1, Summary Statistics (Washington, D.C.: Government Printing Office, 1961): pp. 11-2 through 11-20, the paper industry (SIC 26) has the highest ratio--by far --of water consumption to value added of all two-digit SIC industries in 1954. All other resource intensities are inferred from inspection of "The Transactions Table of the 1958 Input-Output Study and Revised Direct Total Requirements Data," Survey of Current Business 45 (September, 1965): 33-49 as well as from perusal of descriptions of major SIC groups in U.S. Bureau of the Census, 1963 Census of Manufactures, vol. 2, Industry Statistics, parts 1 and 2 (Washington, D.C.: Government Printing Office, 1966).

pairs of endowment and output ratio lists are presented in table 2.
Spearman's r can range in value from -1 to +1, with values approachin
+1 as positive rank correlation increases.[1] Values of r less than
0.42 (for nine regions) are significant at a less than 85 percent
level.[2]

Interpretation of Test Results

The first set of tests (rows 1-3 in table 2) treats endowments
and industries in highly aggregated forms. Regional endowments
are represented by average values of the regions' resource products
in three major categories: (1) agriculture and fishery products,
(2) forest products, and (3) mine, well, and quarry products. The
outputs are represented by the aggregate value added by the three
groups of industries which use the three categories of resource
products intensively as raw inputs: (1) food (Standard Industrial
Classification or SIC 20) and textiles (SIC 22); (2) lumber and wood
products (SIC 24) and pulp and paper products (SIC 26); (3) chemicals
(SIC 28), petroleum and coal products (SIC 29), stone, clay, and
glass products (SIC 32), and primary metal industries (SIC 33).

The rank correlation coefficients of these ratios are solid
evidence that the production of the endowment-output result (26)
is accurate for the United States space-economy in a fundamental
way. For broadly defined types of resources and goods, regions do
produce their natural resource-derived products in proportions that
reflect their comparative advantages, i.e., their resource endowment
proportions.

The second set of tests (rows 4-6 of table 2) involves much les
data aggregation that the first set. The endowments are those for
which usable physical data--as opposed to primary processing value
data--are conveniently available: timber (forest land area), water
supply (an index of average regional runoff), and petroleum (estimate
reserves). The industries are those which are presumed to use the
resources highly intensively: lumber and wood (SIC 24), pulp and
paper (SIC 26), and petroleum and coal products (SIC 29).

Here again, the endowment-output result (26) is supported by
the data. Columns 7 through 12 in appendix A show that the rankings
of forest-petroleum ratios are very nearly the same as the rankings
of water-petroleum ratios; so the timber and water endowment effects
tend to merge when paired with petroleum. On the other hand, row 4

---

[1] E. G. Olds, "Distributions of Sums of Squares of Rank Differences for
Small Numbers of Individuals," Annals of Mathematical Statistics 9 (1938): 133-48

[2] Ibid., table IV.

of table 2 shows that timber and water effects on, respectively, the wood and the paper industries can be separated. Indeed, the relatively high rank correlation between the wood-paper industry ratio and the forest-water supply ratio is perplexing since pulp is also assumed to be relatively intensive in forest resource products, whereas the model predicts that result (26) is most likely to be observed when the goods under study exhibit contrasting factor intensities. It is possibile that the prediction holds up because water is so much the predominant input in the paper industry while the wood industry exhibits a low intensity in the use of water.

A third set of tests (rows 7-21 in table 2) aims at bringing out some of the output proportions of individual industries that are aggregated in the first set of tests. The general resource category of mine, well, and quarry products is broken down into metals, petroleum, and non-metallic minerals. This way, the petroleum, and the primary metal industries or the food and the stone and clay products industries can be compared in ratios. The endowments of minerals are represented by average values of the regions' resource products in four categories: (1) clay, gypsum, sand and gravel, and stone; (2) crude petroleum; (3) coal and iron; (4) copper, lead, and zinc. Coal is included with iron because it is used intensively in iron and steel production.

It is perhaps noteworthy that the basic results for the wood industry (SIC 24) in comparison to the metallic and non-metallic industries (SIC 33 and 32) are invariant for two different measures of forest endowment. The 1947 and 1958 tests (rows 12 and 14 in table 2) use the historical average values of aggregated resource production, while the 1967 tests (rows 13 and 15) use the forest land areas for 1963. This modest evidence for robustness suggests the validity of using the historical average value as a measure of natural resource endowment.

Ten out of the thirty-three tests in the third set produce r values with less than 85 percent significance levels (rows 8, 11, 16, 20, and 21). With one exception (row 16), even the low r values are still positive, which is as result (26) predicts.

The interregional model that generates result (26) allows for complexity and indeterminacy in the endowment-output relation when there are multiple goods being produced with multiple factors.[1]

---

[1] See chapter V above.

76

TABLE 2

EMPIRICAL TEST RESULTS: SPEARMAN'S COEFFICIENT OF RANK CORRELATION (r) FOR SELECTED INDUSTRY AND RESOURCE RATIOS

	Output Ratio	Endowment Ratio	1947 Columns in App. B & A	1947 r	1958 Columns in App. B & A	1958 r	1967 Columns in App. B & A	1967 r
1	Food & Textiles[a] / Lumber & Paper Products	Value Extracted Ag. & Fish. / Value Extracted Forest	B1:A1	0.57	B2:A1	0.53	.	.
2	Food & Textiles[a] / Chemical, Petroleum, Stone-Clay-Glass, Metal Products	Value Extracted Ag. & Fish. / Value Extracted Minerals	B3:A2	0.70	B4:A2	0.65	.	.
3	Lumber & Paper Products / Chemical, Petroleum, Stone-Clay-Glass, Metal Products	Value Extracted Forest / Value Extracted Minerals	B5:A3	0.87	B6:A3	0.80	.	.
4	Lumber Products / Paper Products	Forest Land Area / Water Supply	B7:A4	0.48	B8:A5	0.47	B9:A6	0.67
5	Lumber Products / Petroleum Products	Forest Land Area / Petroleum Reserves	B10:A7	0.42	B11:A8	0.58	B12:A9	0.65
6	Paper Products / Petroleum Products	Water Supply / Petroleum Reserves	B13:A10	0.85	B14:A11	0.96	B15:A12	0.87
7	Food Products / Lumber Products	Value Extracted Ag. & Fish. / Value Extracted Forest	B16:A1	0.80	B17:A1	0.82	.	.
8	Food Products / Paper Products	Value Extracted Ag. & Fish. / Water Supply	B18:A13	0.12	B19:A13	0.32	.	.
9	Food Products / Petroleum Products	Value Extracted Ag. & Fish. / Value Extracted Petroleum	B20:A14	0.87	B21:A14	0.95	.	.

#	Output Industries	Endowment Ratios						
10	Food Products / Stone-Clay-Glass Products	Value Extracted Ag. & Fish. / Value Extracted Non-Metallic	B22:A15	0.78	B23:A15	0.65	. . .	. . .
11	Food Products / Primary Metal Products	Value Extracted Ag. & Fish. / Value Extracted Coal & Metal	B24:A16	0.35	B25:A16	0.53	. . .	. . .
12	Lumber Products / Stone-Clay-Glass Products	Value Extracted Forest / Value Extracted Non-Metallic	B26:A17	0.88	B27:A17	0.82	. . .	. . .
13	Lumber Products / Stone-Clay-Glass Products	Forest Land Area / Value Extracted Non-Metallic	. . .	. . .	. . .	. . .	B28:A18	0.76[b]
14	Lumber Products / Primary Metal Products	Value Extracted Forest / Value Extracted Coal & Metal	B29:A19	0.55	B30:A19	0.42	. . .	. . .
15	Lumber Products / Primary Metal Products	Forest Land Area / Value Extracted Coal & Metal	. . .	. . .	. . .	. . .	B31:A20	0.43
16	Paper Products / Stone-Clay-Glass Products	Water Supply / Value Extracted Non-Metallic	B32:A21	0.18	B33:A21	0.00	B34:A22	0.36[b]
17	Paper Products / Primary Metal Products	Water Supply / Value Extracted Coal & Metal	B35:A23	0.65	B36:A23	0.57	B37:A24	0.42
18	Petroleum Products / Stone-Clay-Glass Products	Value Extracted Petroleum / Value Extracted Non-Metallic	B38:A25	0.63	B39:A25	0.90	B40:A26	0.95[b]
19	Petroleum Products / Primary Metal Products	Value Extracted Petroleum / Value Extracted Coal, Metal	B41:A27	0.88	B42:A27	0.90	B43:A28	0.86
20	Stone-Clay-Glass Products / Primary Metal Products	Value Extracted Non-Metallic / Value Extracted Coal, Metal	B44:A29	0.33	B45:A29	0.35	B46:A30	0.26[b]
21	Iron & Steel Products / Nonferrous Metal Products	Value Extracted Coal, Iron / Value Extracted Base Metal	. . .	. . .	B47:A31	0.28	B48:A32	0.83

NOTE: The relevant lists of endowment and output ratios are indicated in the column to the left of the r value. Hence, "B7:A4" means that the coefficient measures the correlation of column 7 in appendix B with column 4 in appendix A.

[a] The 1947 ratio includes value added by the leather industry (SIC 31). The 1958 ratio includes value added by the leather industry and tobacco industry (SIC 21).

[b] Eight regions observed.

There seems no indisputable way to judge what significance level is scientifically acceptable or what proportion of "significant" coefficients represents adequate support for result (26) in the third testing approach. Given that all the correlation coefficients based on broadly defined industries and resources (rows 1-3 in Table 2) test at better than a 90 percent significance level,[1] and given that all the coefficients based on physical definitions of resources (rows 4-6) test at better than 85 percent, it seems reasonable to assert that result (26) is not refuted by some lower coefficients among the remaining tests (rows 7-21). Without attempting ad hoc explanations of why some correlations are not high, it must be remembered that the model concedes that the complexity of a sophisticated multi-good, multi-factor space-economy may obscure the endowment-output effect. Nevertheless, it can fairly be said that the general impression conveyed by table 2 is that output proportions of resource-based industries are often correlated with endowment proportions of regional natural[2] resources.

---

[1] See the preceding section of this chapter on statistical procedure.

[2] Natural resource supplies were chosen for testing because they were assumed to be sufficiently inelastic and immobile as to be exogenous. An example of when resource endowments are likely to be more endogenous is the case of labor supplies. It could be argued that, within the United States, population is mobile among regions and that a regional industry requiring well-educated workers can attract them from outside the region if the indigenous labor force is too poorly educated. In this case, regional resource (i.e., labor) endowments are inelastic and immobile only in the very short run; so the direction of causation in result (26) is ambiguous. Nevertheless, the H-O-J/W-T-M model is based on the general equilibrium assumption of efficient allocation of resources (see chapter VI above). Hence, testing whether the ratio of uneducated to educated labor supplies correlates with the ratio of uneducated labor-intensive to educated labor-intensive industrial outputs would give some measure of the extent to which interregional production differences in the United States reflect an efficient allocation of labor.

Appendix C lists the data necessary for such a test. The percentage of people in a state over age twenty-five having fewer than five years of education is divided by the percentage of people having at least four years of high school. This ratio is taken as the index of the state's uneducated-educated labor endowment proportions. The 1972 Census of Manufactures indicates that the textile and apparel industries (SIC 22 and 23) exhibit the highest ratio of number of production workers to non-production workers (supervisory, technical, sales, clerical), while the chemical industry (SIC 28) exhibits one of the lowest production to non-production worker ratios. On the assumption that production workers require relatively less education for their jobs than non-production workers, result (26) preducts that the ratio of value added by the textile and apparel industries to value added by the chemical industry in a state will be positively correlated with the state's ratio of uneducated to educated populations.

In fact, the Spearman coefficient of rank correlation for the ratios in appendix C is +0.33, which is significant at the 95 percent level for a sample size of 40. This test illustrates the ability of the H-O-J/W-T-M model to associate resources with the geography of production even when resource supplies are elastic and mobile enough to impose relatively mild, short-run limits on regional production possibilities.

Conclusions about Using the Model

The purpose of this chapter has been more illustrative than definitive: the tests of result (26) were presented to illustrate the fact that the theory embodied in the H-O-J/W-T-M model and its interregional special case are capable of yielding concrete predictions about an actually existing pattern of industrial location. In that way the model has been demonstrated to fulfill part of the task of theory in positivist social science: abstracting from reality in order to make empirically testable predictions about reality.[1]

Another part of the task of theory is predicting accurately, i.e., generating hypotheses that can be accepted on the basis of empirical tests. Here, too, the model's capabilities have been demonstrated--at least in cases of United States regional industries and natural resources in the 1940s, 1950s and 1960s. The model's trade-theoretic prediction of the effect of resource proportions on industrial output proportions has been supported in more test cases than not; so the tests have yielded some information about the industrial geography of the United States.

The test results might also be taken as indicating more than just a relationship between endowment ratios in the United States. As was discussed in chapter VI, the H-O-J/W-T-M model and its interregional special case are designed to analyze industrial location in an economy characterized by general equilibrium with efficient allocation of resources. Support of a specific hypothesis of the model, e.g., support of result (26), may therefore be construed as some evidence of the efficiency of the United States space-economy.

The relative success of the tests should in some part be imputed to their methodology. Unlike most previous tests of the factor endowments hypothesis, the present tests use resource proportions to predict output proportions rather than concentration ratios or location quotients. This means looking for comparative advantage, as reflected in natural resource proportions, to be reflected in output proportions, whatever the absolute output levels (concentration ratios). For example, column 2 of appendix A shows the Middle Atlantic and Mountain regions to have similar comparative advantages with respect to agricultural and mineral resources.

---

[1] Milton Friedman, "The Methodology of Positive Economics" in *Essays in Positive Economics*, (Chicago: University of Chicago Press, 1953), pp. 3-43.

The Middle Atlantic is a much more industrialized region; yet columns 3 and 4 of appendix B show that the Middle Atlantic and Mountain regions have similar industrial profiles, i.e., produce agriculture-based goods and minerals-based goods in similar proportions. Despite great differences in their concentration ratios, the regions reveal a similarity that is predicted by the model.

The selection for testing of goods exhibiting contrasting factor intensities follows directly from the generalization of the two-factor, two-good model in chapters IV and V and gives the tests a greater chance of detecting the endowment-output relation in a complex multi-factor, multi-good economy. Finally, the use of a non-parametric statistical measure reduces the potential biases due to omitted variables while it still addresses the essentially ordinal relationship predicted by the model.

CHAPTER VIII

SUMMARY OF THE MONOGRAPH

This monograph has presented an empirically testable model of
industrial location by proceding from development of a general
intraregional and interregional theory, through derivation of an
interregional case of the general theory, to an empirical test of
the interregional case. Assuming no interregional resource mobility
and holding market locations and prices constant, the main properties of the model derive from variations in geographic parameters:
differences among regions in their endowments of inputs, distances
between input and production sites and between production sites
and output markets. The assumption of fixed factor endowments
renders the model a theory of the short-run in which factor supply
reactions are minor. The assumption of fixed prices and markets
holds demand constant and thereby renders the model a theory of
production rather than market location.

A criticism of Weber[1] for neglecting the effect of transport
costs on site rent has led to the incorporation of Thünen's analysis of rent[2] into the least-cost location model. The observation
that Weber predicts which location will produce given goods while
Ohlin[3] predicts which goods will be produced by given locations
has been formalized in a nonlinear programming model. The duality
properties of this model constitute a formal demonstration that
cases in location theory that assume finite resources and constant
demand can also be addressed as cases in trade theory. The assumption of finite and interregionally immobile factors provides a
clear basis for distinguishing among regions according to production
possibilities. Holding the demand facing each region constant in
the form of fixed prices allows trade theory to work as a theory of
location without being burdened with explaining why a region exports
some of what it produces rather than consuming it at home.

---

[1] Weber, Location of Industries.

[2] Thünen, Isolated State.

[3] Ohlin, Trade.

81

This monograph has also explored a particular version of its general model, i.e., the strictly interregional version wherein intraregional transport costs and, therefore, site rent, are assumed to be zero. This version stresses the trade-theoretic portions of the model by collapsing the regions into points and concentrates on differences among them in terms of factor endowments and distances to world markets. This approach has allowed Jones's model of general equilibrium[1] to be used to predict both the effects of interregional differences in endowments on output proportions and the effects of interregional differences in market access on relative wages under the assumptions of fixed resources and prices.

The applicability of the model to concrete data has been demonstrated by the construction of empirical tests of the model's endowment-output result. United States data have been used to test the interregional model's prediction that if one region possesses relatively more of a factor than another region, it will produce relatively more of a good that uses the abundant factor intensively.

Unlike most (or all) previous tests of the Heckscher-Ohlin trade theory of endowment proportions, the tests in this paper have compared endowment ratios with output _ratios_ instead of with absolute levels of output. Goods with contrasting factor intensities have been compared in order to increase the likelihood of observing the endowment ratio effect in an economy that is much more complex than the two-good, two-factor model in which it is predicted; and, since the ratio predictions are based on a simplified model of the multi-good, multi-factor reality, non-parametric statistical methods have been used to help reduce the danger of misspecifying the true relationships among the observed ratios. The relatively high correlations obtained in many of the tests support the hypothesis that comparative advantage, as measured in the region's ratio of resources, is reflected in its industrial profile, as measured in the region's ratio of outputs.

Since industrial profile is the result of industrial location decisions, the empirical chapter also supports the motivating theme of the whole monograph, namely, that relative locational pull is the same as comparative advantage. Whereas much location theory seeks to determine the absolutely lowest-cost production location for an industry, much trade theory assumes that a given industry

---

[1]R. Jones, "General Equilibrium."

will be located in more than one region, with relative costs and
outputs of different industries varying across regions. The empirical tests of the present study follow trade theory in treating
locational pull more as a matter of the proportions in which industries locate in a region and less as a matter of absolute production
costs. As the interregional version of the general trade/location
model shows, what prevents all plants being pulled only to the
region offering the absolutely lowest cost are the limited production posibilities imposed by finite resources combined with fixed
received output prices. Any output amounts greater than the full-
employment equilibrium amounts implied by the region's production
possibilities will drive the wages of the inelastically supplied
resources up such that factor payments exceed given prices and
some plants must cut back production to avoid negative income. By
investigating comparative rather than absolute advantage, the
empirical tests provide an example of how the location theorist can
practice his trade by putting trade theory into practice.

APPENDICES

APPENDIX A

TABLE 3

ENDOWMENT RATIOS AND RANKS: REGIONAL RESOURCE PROPORTIONS

Regions	1a 1870-1950 Ave. Val. Ag., Fish. / Ave. Val. Forest	Rank	2a 1870-1950 Ave. Val. Ag., Fish. / Ave. Val. Minerals	Rank	3a 1870-1950 Ave. Val. Forest / Ave. Val. Minerals	Rank	4b 1945 Forest Land Area / Water Supply	Rank
New England	6.342	8	9.864	1	1.555	1	0.69	8
Middle Atlantic	17.878	3	1.328	8	0.074	9	0.52	9
East North Central	18.466	2	4.414	4	0.239	5	0.74	6
West North Central	69.542	1	8.865	2	0.127	7	1.08	2
South Atlantic	7.042	6	3.629	5	0.515	4	1.32	1
East South Central	6.959	7	4.650	3	0.668	3	0.72	7
West South Central	10.993	5	1.467	7	0.133	6	1.04	3
Mountain	16.597	4	1.279	9	0.077	8	0.79	5
Pacific	3.210	9	2.411	6	0.751	2	0.85	4

Regions	5c 1953 Forest Land Area / Water Supply	Rank	6d 1963 Forest Land Area / Water Supply	Rank	7e 1945 Forest Land Area / 1947 Petrol.	Rank	8f 1953 Forest Land Area / 1958 Petrol.	Rank
New England	0.68	8	0.70	8	∞	1	∞	1
Middle Atlantic	0.53	9	0.53	9	147.3	4	186.0	3
East North Central	0.80	6	0.78	7	90.2	5	61.1	5
West North Central	1.06	3	1.01	4	74.6	6	31.6	6
South Atlantic	1.40	1	1.43	1	2,744.8	2	2,016.3	2
East South Central	0.75	7	0.79	6	157.8	3	120.7	4
West South Central	1.09	2	1.13	3	3.4	9	2.6	9
Mountain	0.96	4	1.17	2	25.6	7	16.4	7
Pacific	0.85	5	0.86	5	19.0	8	16.2	8

Regions	9[g] 1963 Forest Land Area — 1967 Petrol. Reserves	Rank	10[h] Water Supply — 1947 Petrol. Reserves	Rank	11[i] Water Supply — 1958 Petrol. Reserves	Rank	12[j] Water Supply — 1967 Petrol. Reserves	Rank
New England	∞	1	∞	1	∞	1	∞	1
Middle Atlantic	374.5	3	284	3	353	3	705	3
East North Central	84.6	5	122	5	77	5	109	5
West North Central	40.5	6	69	6	30	6	40	6
South Atlantic	1,911.7	2	2,083	2	1,442	2	1,339	2
East South Central	121.1	4	220	4	160	3	153	4
West South Central	2.6	9	3	9	2	9	2	9
Mountain	22.8	7	32	7	17	7	20	7
Pacific	14.5	8	23	8	19	8	17	8

Regions	13[k] Up to 1950 Ave. Val. Ag., Fish. — Water Supply	Rank	14[l] Up to 1950 Ave. Val. Ag., Fish. — Ave. Val. Petroleum	Rank	15[m] Up to 1950 Ave. Val. Ag., Fish. — Ave. Val. Non-Metal	Rank	16[n] Up to 1950 Ave. Val. Ag., Fish. — Ave. Val. Coal, Metal	Rank
New England	6.73	9	11.24	1	6.42	8	2,679.00	1
Middle Atlantic	14.18	4	11.94	6	3.26	9	0.69	9
East North Central	29.87	2	14.82	5	6.75	7	3.42	5
West North Central	59.05	1	36.04	3	23.25	1	5.78	4
South Atlantic	12.98	5	13.56	2	9.29	6	1.72	7
East South Central	9.41	7	0.59	4	16.70	4	2.04	6
West South Central	21.56	3	3.44	9	22.24	2	22.58	3
Mountain	8.63	8	1.42	7	18.20	3	0.80	8
Pacific	10.03	6		8	9.87	5	23.21	2

TABLE 3--Continued

Regions	17[o] Up to 1950 Ave. Val. Forest — Ave. Val. Non-Metal	Rank	18[p] Up to 1970 1963 Forest Land Area — Ave. Val. Non-Metal	Rank	19[q] Up to 1950 Ave. Val. Forest — Ave. Val. Coal, Metal	Rank	20[r] Up to 1970 1963 Forest Land Area — Ave. Val. Coal, Metal	Rank
New England	1.01	6	0.50	*	422.50	1	22.102	1
Middle Atlantic	0.18	9	0.11	8	0.04	9	0.029	9
East North Central	0.37	7	0.14	7	0.19	6	0.077	7
West North Central	0.33	8	0.28	6	0.08	7	0.082	6
South Atlantic	1.32	4	0.54	4	0.24	5	0.144	4
East South Central	2.40	2	0.81	2	0.29	4	0.128	5
West South Central	2.02	3	0.62	3	2.05	3	1.409	3
Mountain	1.10	5	1.06	1	0.05	8	0.069	8
Pacific	3.07	1	0.47	5	7.23	2	2.407	2

Regions	21[s] Up to 1950 Water Supply — Ave. Val. Non-Metal	Rank	22[t] Up to 1970 Water Supply — Ave. Val. Non-Metal	Rank	23[u] Up to 1950 Water Supply — Ave. Val. Coal, Metal	Rank	24[v] Up to 1970 Water Supply — Ave. Val. Coal, Metal	Rank
New England	0.955	5	0.721	*	39.8230	1	31.62	1
Middle Atlantic	0.230	8	0.212	7	0.0049	9	0.05	9
East North Central	0.226	9	0.178	8	0.0115	6	0.09	6
West North Central	0.394	7	0.280	6	0.0098	7	0.08	7
South Atlantic	0.715	6	0.380	5	0.0132	5	0.10	5
East South Central	1.774	2	1.019	1	0.0217	4	0.16	4
West South Central	1.032	3	0.549	4	0.1047	3	1.25	3
Mountain	2.110	1	0.904	2	0.0092	8	0.06	8
Pacific	0.984	4	0.550	3	0.2313	2	2.81	2

25[w]

Regions	Ave. Val. Petroleum / Ave. Val. Non-Metal	Rank
New England	0.00	9
Middle Atlantic	0.29	7
East North Central	0.56	6
West North Central	1.57	4
South Atlantic	0.26	8
East South Central	1.23	5
West South Central	37.52	1
Mountain	5.30	3
Pacific	6.97	2

26[x]

Regions	Ave. Val. Petroleum / Ave. Val. Non-Metal	Rank
New England	0.00	*
Middle Atlantic	0.22	7
East North Central	0.49	6
West North Central	1.46	4
South Atlantic	0.12	8
East South Central	1.25	5
West South Central	35.16	1
Mountain	5.93	2
Pacific	4.51	3

27[y]

Regions	Ave. Val. Petroleum / Ave. Val. Coal, Metal	Rank
New England	0.00	9
Middle Atlantic	0.06	7
East North Central	0.29	4
West North Central	0.39	3
South Atlantic	0.05	8
East South Central	1.51	6
West South Central	38.23	1
Mountain	0.23	5
Pacific	16.39	2

28[z]

Regions	Ave. Val. Petroleum / Ave. Val. Coal, Metal	Rank
New England	0.00	9
Middle Atlantic	0.06	7
East North Central	0.27	5
West North Central	0.42	3
South Atlantic	0.03	8
East South Central	0.20	6
West South Central	79.87	1
Mountain	0.39	4
Pacific	23.14	2

29[aa]

Regions	Ave. Val. Non-Metal / Ave. Val. Coal, Metal	Rank
New England	417.14	1
Middle Atlantic	0.21	6
East North Central	0.51	4
West North Central	0.25	5
South Atlantic	0.18	7
East South Central	0.12	8
West South Central	1.02	3
Mountain	0.04	9
Pacific	2.35	2

30[bb]

Regions	Ave. Val. Non-Metal / Ave. Val. Coal, Metal	Rank
New England	43.88	*
Middle Atlantic	0.26	6
East North Central	0.56	3
West North Central	0.29	4
South Atlantic	0.27	5
East South Central	0.16	7
West South Central	2.27	2
Mountain	0.07	8
Pacific	5.10	1

31[cc]

Regions	Ave. Val. Coal, Iron / Ave. Val. Base Metal	Rank
New England	55.5	3
Middle Atlantic	130.3	2
East North Central	9.0	5
West North Central	4.7	6
South Atlantic	290.3	1
East South Central	27.8	4
West South Central	2.0	7
Mountain	0.3	9
Pacific	1.2	8

32[dd]

Regions	Ave. Val. Coal, Iron / Ave. Val. Base Metal	Rank
New England	0.1	9
Middle Atlantic	65.0	2
East North Central	9.2	4
West North Central	4.4	5
South Atlantic	250.9	1
East South Central	21.5	3
West South Central	2.3	6
Mountain	0.2	8
Pacific	1.0	7

TABLE 3--Continued

NOTES: The regions are the Geographic Divisions defined in U.S. Bureau of the Census, United States Census of Manufactures: 1958, vol. 3, Area Statistics (Washington, D.C.: Government Printing Office, 1961),viii. See text of chapter VII above. Sources of the ratios are identified in the foot-notes to specific columns.

The data attributed to Mineral Resources of the United States 1910, Mineral Resources of the United States, 1930, Minerals Yearbook 1950, and Minerals Yearbook 1970 include only amounts that are listed by states. Sometimes resources are extracted but the tonnages and values are not revealed. If the data for another recent year are revealed they are used in place of the secret data; otherwise, these data are excluded from the table. If tonnages but not values are revealed, the value is computed on the basis of a per-ton price in a neighboring state in which the value is revealed.

The values attributed to Perloff, et al., Regions, pp. 638-41 are for five years: 1870, 1890, 1910, 1930, and 1950. A deflated historical average of these values is computed:

Average Value of Resource i Extracted $= \frac{1}{5} \sum_k \frac{R_i^k}{p^k}$, where k = 1870, 1890, 1910, 1930, or 1950.

R_i^k is the value from Perloff, et al., Regions for year k and p^k is the wholesale price level for year k, as reported in U.S. Bureau of the Census, Historical Statistics of the United States, series 23 (Washington, D.C.: Government Printing Office, 1975), p. 199. The average values in columns headed "Up to 1950" are based on data from the three years 1910, 1930, and 1950. Hence the average is computed:

Average Value of Resource i Extracted $= \frac{1}{3} \sum_k \frac{R_i^k}{p^k}$, where k = 1910, 1930, or 1950.

The average values in columns headed "Up to 1970" are based on data from the years 1910, 1930, 1950, and 1970. Hence, the average is computed:

Average Value of Resource i Extracted $= \frac{1}{4} \sum_k \frac{R_i^k}{p^k}$, where k = 1910, 1930, 1950, or 1970.

*New England is not ranked because the 1967 Census of Manufactures contains insufficient data on the output of the stone-clay-glass industry (SIC 32), which is intensive in non-metallic ores.

aColumns 1, 2, 3: values of extracted resources are from Harvey S. Perloff, Edgar S. Dunn, Jr., Eric E. Lampard, and Richard F. Muth, Regions, Resources, and Economic Growth (Baltimore: Johns Hopkins Press, 1960), pp. 638-41.

bColumn 4: commercial forest land areas (in thousands of acres) are from U.S. Forest Service, Forests and National Prosperity, Miscellaneous Pub. 668 (Reappraisal Report) Washington, D.C.: Government Printing Office, 1948). Water supply for each region is the sum of the average (1931-1960) runoffs of each basin in the region divided by the number of basins in the region. The average runoff amounts (in millions of gallons per day) as well as the basin definitions, are taken from U.S. Geological Survey, Estimated Use of Water in the United States, 1965, by C. Richard Murray, Circular 556 (Washington, D.C.: U.S. Department of the Interior, 1968), pp. v and 53.

cColumn 5: commercial forest land areas (in thousands of acres) are from U.S. Forest Service, Timber Resources for America's Future, Forest Resource Report No. 14 (Washington, D.C.: Government Printing Office, 1958). Water supplies are from the same source as in footnote b.

dColumn 6: commercial forest land areas (in thousands of acres) are from U.S. Forest Service, Timber Trends in the United States (Washington, D.C.: Government Printing Office, 1965). Water supplies are from the same source as in footnote b.

eColumn 7: forest land areas are from the same source as in footnote b. Petroleum reserves (in millions of barrels) are from U.S. Bureau of Mines, Minerals Yearbook 1950 (Washington, D.C.: Government Printing Office, 1953), p. 884.

fColumn 8: forest land areas are from the same source as in footnote c. Petroleum reserves (in millions of barrels) are from U.S. Bureau of Mines, Minerals Yearbook 1958, vol. 2, Fuels (Washington, D.C.: Government Printing Office, 1959), p. 356.

gColumn 9: forest land areas are from the same source as in footnote d. Petroleum reserves (in millions of barrels) are from U.S. Bureau of Mines, Minerals Yearbook 1970, vol. 1, Metals, Minerals, and Fuels (Washington, D.C.: Government Printing Office, 1972), p. 836.

hColumn 10: water supplies are from the same source as in footnote b. Petroleum reserves are from the same source as in footnote e.

iColumn 11: water supplies are from the same source as in footnote b. Petroleum reserves are from the same source as in footnote f.

TABLE 3--Continued

[j]Column 12: water supplies are from the same source as in footnote g.

[k]Column 13: agriculture and fishery values are from Perloff, et al., Regions, as cited in footnote a. Water supplies are from the same source as in footnote b.

[l]Column 14: agriculture and fishery values are from the same source as in footnote k. Petroleum values are from U.S. Geological Survey, Mineral Resources of the United States, 1910, part 1, Metals (Washington, D.C.: Government Printing Office, 1911), pp. 43-57; U.S. Bureau of Mines, Mineral Resources of the United States 1930, part 1, Metals (Washington D.C.: Government Printing Office, 1933), A93-A119; U.S. Bureau of Mines, Minerals Yearbook 1950 (Washington, D.C.: Government Printing Office, 1953), pp. 42-72.

[m]Column 15: agriculture and fishery values are from the same source as in footnote a. Non-metallic ore (clay, gypsum, sand and gravel, stone) values are from precisely the same sources as petroleum values in footnote l.

[n]Column 16: agriculture and fishery values are from the same source as in footnote a. Coal and metallic ore (copper, iron, lead, zinc) values are from precisely the same sources as petroleum values in footnote l.

[o]Column 17: forest values are from Perloff, et al., Regions as cited in footnote a. Non-metallic ore (clay, gypsum, sand and gravel, stone) values are from precisely the same sources as petroleum values in footnote l.

[p]Column 18: commercial forest land areas are from the same source as in footnote d. Non-metallic ore (clay, gypsum, sand and gravel, stone) values are from the same sources as petroleum values in foot-note l plus another source, U.S. Bureau of Mines, Minerals Yearbook 1970, vol. 1, Metals, Minerals and Fuels (Washington, D.C.: Government Printing Office, 1972), pp. 111-31.

[q]Column 19: commercial forest values are from the same source as in footnote o. Coal and metallic ore (copper, iron, lead, zinc) values are from precisely the same sources as petroleum values in footnote l.

[r]Column 20: commercial forest land areas are from the same source as in footnote d. Coal and metallic ore (copper, iron, lead, zinc) values are from precisely the same sources as non-metallic ore values in footnote p.

sColumn 21: water supplies are from the same source as footnote b. Non-metallic ore (clay, gypsum, sand and gravel, stone) values are from precisely the same sources as petroleum values in footnote 1.

tColumn 22: water supplies are from the same source as in footnote b. Non-metallic ore (clay, gypsum, sand and gravel, stone) values are from the same sources as in footnote p.

uColumn 23: water supplies are from the same source as in footnote b. Coal and metallic ore (copper, iron, lead, zinc) values are from precisely the same sources as petroleum values in footnote 1.

vColumn 24: water supplies are from the same source as in footnote b. Coal and metallic ore (copper, iron, lead, zinc) values are from precisely the same sources as non-metallic ore values in footnote p.

wColumn 25: petroleum values are from the same sources as in footnote 1. Non-metallic ore (clay, gypsum, sand and gravel, stone) values are from precisely the same sources as petroleum values in footnote 1.

xColumn 26: petroleum values are from precisely the same sources as non-metallic ore values in footnote p. Non-metallic ore (clay, gypsum, sand and gravel, stone) values are from the same sources as in footnote p.

yColumn 27: petroleum values are from the same sources as in footnote 1. Coal and metallic ore (copper, iron, lead, zinc) values are from precisely the same sources as petroleum values in footnote 1.

zColumn 28: petroleum, coal, and metallic ore (copper, iron, lead, zinc) values are all from precisely the same sources as non-metallic ore values in footnote p.

aaColumn 29: non-metallic ore (clay, gypsum, sand and gravel, stone), coal, and metallic ore (copper, iron, lead, zinc) values are all from precisely the same sources as petroleum values in footnote 1.

bbColumn 30: non-metallic ore (clay, gypsum, sand and gravel, stone) values are from the same sources as in footnote p. Coal and metallic ore (copper, iron, lead, zinc) values are from precisely the same sources as non-metallic ore values in footnote p.

ccColumn 31: Coal, iron ore, base metal ore (copper, lead, zinc) values are all from precisely the same sources as petroleum values in footnote 1.

ddColumn 32: coal, iron ore, and base metal ore (copper, lead, zinc) values are all from precisely the same sources as non-metallic ore values in footnote p.

APPENDIX B

TABLE 4

OUTPUT RATIOS AND RANKS: REGIONAL VALUE ADDED PROPORTION BY
STANDARD INDUSTRIAL CLASSIFICATION (SIC)

Regions	1 — 1947 Val. Add. SIC 20,22,31 / SIC 24,26	Rank	2 — 1958 Val. Add. SIC 20,21,22,31 / SIC 24,26	Rank	3 — 1947 Val. Add. SIC 20,22,31 / SIC 28,29,32,33	Rank
New England	4.02	3	2.56	6	3.19	1
Middle Atlantic	4.29	2	3.67	3	0.81	7
East North Central	2.81	5	2.79	5	0.59	8
West North Central	6.75	1	5.54	1	2.03	2
South Atlantic	4.01	4	4.21	4	1.98	3
East South Central	2.36	7	2.82	2	1.27	4
West South Central	1.52	8	2.16	8	0.55	9
Mountain	2.36	6	2.44	7	0.84	6
Pacific	1.06	9	1.34	9	1.23	5

Regions	4 — 1958 Val. Add. SIC 20,21,22,31 / SIC 28,29,32,33	Rank	5 — 1947 Val. Add. SIC 24,26 / SIC 28,29,32,33	Rank	6 — 1958 Val. Add. SIC 24,26 / SIC 28,29,32,33	Rank
New England	1.74	1	0.79	2	0.680	2
Middle Atlantic	0.65	7	0.19	9	0.176	9
East North Central	0.52	8	0.21	8	0.187	8
West North Central	1.57	2	0.30	7	0.283	6
South Atlantic	1.49	5	0.49	4	0.354	4
East South Central	0.83	3	0.54	3	0.293	3
West South Central	0.41	9	0.36	5	0.190	7
Mountain	0.70	6	0.37	6	0.285	5
Pacific	1.02	4	1.17	1		

Regions	7 — 1947 Val. Add. SIC 24/SIC 26	Rank	8 — 1958 Val. Add. SIC 24/SIC 26	Rank	9 — 1967 Val. Add. SIC 24/SIC 26	Rank	10 — 1947 Val. Add. SIC 24/SIC 29	Rank	11 — 1958 Val. Add. SIC 24/SIC 29	Rank
New England	0.29	8	0.23	8	0.23	8	3.43	4	6.14	1
Middle Atlantic	0.19	9	0.17	9	0.17	9	0.28	9	0.70	7
East North Central	0.34	7	0.25	7	0.26	7	0.60	7	0.67	8
West North Central	0.62	6	0.43	6	0.31	6	0.97	6	0.86	6
South Atlantic	1.23	5	0.54	5	0.46	5	8.00	1	5.23	3
East South Central	2.37	3	0.78	3	0.70	3	4.69	2	5.29	2
West South Central	1.73	4	0.62	4	0.63	4	0.47	8	0.25	9
Mountain	21.42	1	4.07	1	2.80	1	1.96	5	1.61	5
Pacific	3.44	2	2.02	2	1.63	2	4.00	3	3.56	4

Regions	12 — 1967 Val. Add. SIC 24/SIC 29	Rank	13 — 1947 Val. Add. SIC 26/SIC 29	Rank	14 — 1958 Val. Add. SIC 26/SIC 29	Rank	15 — 1967 Val. Add. SIC 26/SIC 29	Rank	16 — 1947 Val. Add. SIC 20/SIC 24	Rank
New England	6.12	1	11.74	1	25.16	1	26.30	1	3.15	4
Middle Atlantic	0.52	7	1.42	6	4.00	4	3.10	6	13.42	2
East North Central	0.62	6	1.80	4	2.63	5	5.28	3	9.16	3
West North Central	0.59	8	1.57	5	2.02	6	4.33	5	15.64	1
South Atlantic	3.94	2	6.52	2	9.63	2	8.54	2	1.82	8
East South Central	3.33	3	1.98	3	6.81	3	4.75	4	1.84	7
West South Central	0.17	9	0.27	8	0.41	8	0.27	9	2.20	6
Mountain	1.75	5	0.09	9	0.39	9	0.63	8	2.41	5
Pacific	2.46	4	1.16	7	1.76	7	1.51	7	1.28	9

TABLE 4--Continued

Regions	17 1958 Val. Add. SIC 20/SIC 24	Rank	18 1947 Val. Add. SIC 20/SIC 26	Rank	19 1958 Val. Add. SIC 20/SIC 26	Rank	20 1947 Val. Add. SIC 20/SIC 29	Rank	21 1958 Val. Add. SIC 20/SIC 29	Rank
New England	4.95	5	0.92	9	1.16	9	10.78	3	29.19	1
Middle Atlantic	16.73	2	2.61	7	2.92	6	3.72	8	11.68	5
East North Central	12.23	3	3.07	6	3.09	5	5.53	5	8.14	6
West North Central	16.86	1	9.65	2	7.17	2	15.18	1	14.51	4
South Atlantic	3.98	6	2.23	8	2.16	8	14.54	2	20.81	2
East South Central	3.53	7	4.37	4	2.74	7	8.63	4	18.69	3
West South Central	5.22	4	3.80	5	3.26	4	1.03	9	1.32	9
Mountain	2.92	8	51.57	1	11.87	1	4.71	7	4.68	8
Pacific	1.92	9	4.38	3	3.88	3	5.09	6	6.84	7

Regions	22 1947 Val. Add. SIC 20/SIC 32	Rank	23 1958 Val. Add. SIC 20/SIC 32	Rank	24 1947 Val. Add. SIC 20/SIC 33	Rank	25 1958 Val. Add. SIC 20/SIC 33	Rank	26 1947 Val. Add. SIC 24/SIC 32	Rank
New England	3.36	7	3.28	5	1.27	7	1.42	5	1.07	6
Middle Atlantic	2.77	8	2.78	8	1.06	8	1.09	8	0.21	9
East North Central	3.46	6	2.74	9	0.99	9	0.96	9	0.38	8
West North Central	8.10	1	4.86	1	10.48	1	8.08	1	0.52	7
South Atlantic	2.66	9	2.80	7	2.16	4	1.95	4	1.47	5
East South Central	5.64	4	3.31	3	1.77	5	1.27	7	3.06	3
West South Central	5.50	5	3.01	6	6.18	2	2.76	3	2.50	4
Mountain	7.69	2	3.28	4	1.40	6	1.41	6	3.20	2
Pacific	6.24	3	4.26	2	4.28	3	3.23	2	4.89	1

Table — columns 27–31

Regions	27 — 1958 Val. Add. SIC 24/SIC 32	Rank	28 — 1967 Val. Add. SIC 24/SIC 32	Rank	29 — 1947 Val. Add. SIC 24/SIC 33	Rank	30 — 1958 Val. Add. SIC 24/SIC 33	Rank	31 — 1967 Val. Add. SIC 24/SIC 33	Rank
New England	0.66	5	a		0.49	7	.286	7	0.23	7
Middle Atlantic	0.17	9	0.16	8	0.08	9	0.065	9	0.06	9
East North Central	0.22	8	0.26	7	0.12	8	0.078	8	0.07	8
West North Central	0.24	7	0.35	6	0.67	5	0.479	5	0.37	6
South Atlantic	0.70	4	0.63	5	1.19	3	0.489	3	0.53	2
East South Central	0.94	3	1.06	3	0.96	4	0.358	6	0.44	5
West South Central	0.58	6	0.65	4	3.80	1	0.529	2	0.46	4
Mountain	1.13	2	1.40	2	0.58	6	0.482	4	0.52	3
Pacific	2.22	1	2.16	1	3.35	2	1.684	1	1.30	1

Table — columns 32–36

Regions	32 — 1947 Val. Add. SIC 26/SIC 32	Rank	33 — 1958 Val. Add. SIC 26/SIC 32	Rank	34 — 1967 Val. Add. SIC 26/SIC 32	Rank	35 — 1947 Val. Add. SIC 26/SIC 33	Rank	36 — 1958 Val. Add. SIC 26/SIC 33	Rank
New England	3.66	1	2.83	1	a		1.38	2	1.22	1
Middle Atlantic	1.06	7	0.95	5	0.97	7	0.41	6.5	0.37	7
East North Central	1.13	6	0.89	7	0.99	6	0.32	8	0.31	8
West North Central	0.84	8	0.68	8	1.13	4	1.09	5	1.13	2
South Atlantic	1.19	5	1.29	2	1.37	2	0.97	6.5	0.90	3
East South Central	1.29	4	1.21	3	1.51	1	1.62	1	0.46	6
West South Central	1.45	2	0.92	6	1.03	5	0.41	6.5	0.85	4
Mountain	0.15	9	0.28	9	0.50	8	0.03	9	0.19	9
Pacific	1.42	3	1.10	4	1.33	3	0.98	4	0.83	5

TABLE 4--Continued

Regions	37 1967 Val. Add. SIC 26/SIC 33	Rank	38 1947 Val. Add. SIC 29/SIC 32	Rank	39 1958 Val. Add. SIC 29/SIC 32	Rank	40 1967 Val. Add. SIC 29/SIC 32	Rank	41 1947 Val. Add. SIC 29/SIC 33	Rank
New England	0.99	3	0.31	8	0.11	9	a		0.12	9
Middle Atlantic	0.35	7	0.75	4	0.24	6	0.31	7	0.29	5
East North Central	0.28	8	0.63	6	0.34	4	0.42	5	0.18	7
West North Central	1.20	1	0.53	7	0.33	5	0.59	4	0.69	3
South Atlantic	1.14	2	0.18	9	0.13	8	0.16	8	0.15	8
East South Central	0.62	6	0.65	5	0.18	7	0.32	6	0.21	6
West South Central	0.73	5	5.36	1	2.28	1	3.77	1	6.02	1
Mountain	0.19	9	1.63	2	0.70	2	0.80	3	0.30	4
Pacific	0.80	4	1.22	3	0.62	3	0.88	2	0.84	2

Regions	42 1958 Val. Add. SIC 29/SIC 33	Rank	43 1967 Val. Add. SIC 29/SIC 33	Rank	44 1947 Val. Add. SIC 32/SIC 33	Rank	45 1958 Val. Add. SIC 32/SIC 33	Rank	46 1967 Val. Add. SIC 32/SIC 33	Rank
New England	0.05	9	0.038	9	0.376	6	0.43	5	a	
Middle Atlantic	0.09	6.5	0.113	8	0.383	5	0.39	7	0.36	7
East North Central	0.12	5	0.118	7	0.285	8	0.35	9	0.28	8
West North Central	0.56	2	0.625	2	1.294	1	1.66	1	1.07	1
South Atlantic	0.09	6.5	0.134	5	0.811	3	0.70	4	0.84	2
East South Central	0.07	8	0.131	6	3.14	7	0.38	8	0.41	5
West South Central	2.09	1	2.670	1	1.122	2	0.92	2	0.71	3
Mountain	0.30	4	0.299	4	0.182	9	0.43	6	0.37	6
Pacific	0.47	3	0.528	3	0.686	4	0.76	3	0.60	4

	47		48	
	1958 Val. Add.[b]		1967 Val. Add.[b]	
Regions	SIC 331,2 / SIC 333,4,5,6	Rank	SIC 331,2 / SIC 333,4,5,6	Rank
New England	0.45	9	0.439	9
Middle Atlantic	4.03	4	3.068	1
East North Central	11.43	1	3.008	2
West North Central	4.80	2	1.215	5
South Atlantic	4.18	3	1.916	4
East South Central	2.84	5	1.970	3
West South Central	0.63	8	0.646	8
Mountain	1.84	7	0.686	7
Pacific	2.46	6	0.855	6

SOURCES: 1947 Value Added: U.S. Bureau of the Census, Census of Manufactures: 1947, vol. 3, Statistics by States (Washington, D.C.: Government Printing Office, 1948), pp. 50-51; 1958 Value Added: U.S. Bureau of the Census, United States Census of Manufactures: 1958, vol. 3, Area Statistics (Washington, D.C.: Government Printing Office, 1961), pp. 60-113; 1967 Value Added: U.S. Bureau of the Census, United States Census of Manufactures: 1967, vol. 3, Area Statistics, part 1, Alabama-Montana (Washington, D.C.: Government Printing Office, 1971), pp. 82-157.

NOTES: The regions are the Geographic Divisions defined in U.S. Bureau of the Census, United States Census of Manufactures: 1958, vol. 3, Area Statistics (Washington, D.C.: Government Printing Office, 1961), p. vii. See text of chapter VII above.

Table 1 in the text of chapter VII lists the products represented by each Standard Industrial Classification (SIC) code.

The 1967 values added for the Pacific region have been decreased by the values added in Alaska and Hawaii, whenever such data are revealed.

[a]Insufficient data for SIC 32 are revealed by the 1967 Census of Manufactures for New England.

[b]When insufficient data are revealed by the Census of Manufactures for 3-digit codes under SIC 33 (e.g., SIC 332), then the values are derived by subtracting the sum of all listed 3-digit values from the total value added for SIC 33. When there are insufficient data for subtracting, the value added of the previous Census is used.

TABLE 5

STATE RATIOS OF UNEDUCATED TO EDUCATED LABOR ENDOWMENTS
AND STATE RATIOS OF PRODUCTION WORKER-INTENSIVE TO NON-PRODUCTION
WORKER-INTENSIVE INDUSTRIAL OUTPUTS

State	Val. Add. SIC 22 & 23 Val. Add. SIC 28	Rank	% Population < 5 Yrs. Educ. % Population > 4 Yrs. H.S.	Rank
Alabama	2.126	9	0.2590	7
Arizona	0.736	18	0.1050	15
Arkansas	1.442	14	0.2632	5
California	0.651	21	0.0687	25
Connecticut	0.767	17	0.0768	22
Florida	0.560	23	0.1122	14
Georgia	4.278	5	0.2734	4
Illinois	0.191	32	0.0780	21
Indiana	0.107	34	0.0605	27
Iowa	0.095	35	0.0322	39
Kansas	0.238	29	0.0384	36
Kentucky	0.667	19	0.2442	8
Louisiana	0.060	36	0.3104	2
Maine	8.442	2	0.0512	29
Maryland	0.568	22	0.0860	18
Massachusetts	1.524	13	0.0701	24
Michigan	0.386	26	0.0720	23
Minnesota	0.361	27	0.0417	32
Mississippi	1.590	12	0.3024	3
Montana	0.000	38	0.0456	31
Nebraska	0.238	29	0.0405	34
Nevada	0.000	38	0.0322	39
New Hampshire	8.427	3	0.0417	32
New Jersey	0.287	28	0.0896	17
New York	2.001	10	0.1006	16
North Carolina	4.110	6	0.2597	6
North Dakota	0.000	38	0.0815	20
Ohio	0.224	31	0.0658	26
Oregon	1.016	15	0.0383	37
Pennsylvania	3.303	7	0.0837	19
Rhode Island	4.609	4	0.1164	13
South Carolina	2.563	8	0.3201	1
South Dakota	∞	1	0.0507	30
Tennessee	0.666	20	0.2273	9
Texas	0.188	33	0.1962	10
Vermont	1.944	11	0.0385	35
Virginia	0.952	16	0.1611	12
Washington	0.412	25	0.0346	38
West Virginia	0.044	37	0.1755	11
Wisconsin	0.471	24	0.0587	28

TABLE 5--Continued

SOURCES: Labor force: years of education and high school completed are from U.S. Bureau of the Census, County and City Data Book: 1977 (Washington, D.C.: Government Printing Office, 1978), items 233 and 234; Industry's ratio of number of production workers to all workers is determined from U.S. Bureau of the Census, Census of Manufactures 1972, vol. 3, Area Statistics (Washington, D.C.: Government Printing Office, 1977), "General Summary," table 3; values added are from Bureau of the Census, Census, vol. 3, Area, parts 1 and 2, "States" sections, table 5.

NOTE: The 1972 Census of Manufactures reveals sufficient data for testing only forty states.

SELECTED BIBLIOGRAPHY

Alonso, William. Location and Land Use. Cambridge: Harvard University Press, 1964.

Baldwin, Robert E. "Determinants of the Commodity Structure of U.S. Trade." American Economic Review 61 (1971):126-46.

Balinski, M. L., and Baumol, W. J. "The Dual in Nonlinear Programming and Its Economic Interpretation." Review of Economic Studies 35 (July, 1968):237-56.

Böventer, E. von. "Toward a United Theory of Spatial Economic Structure." Papers, Regional Science Association 10 (1963): 163-87.

Brown, Douglas M. "The Location Decision of the Firm: An Overview of Theory and Evidence." Papers, Regional Science Association 43 (1979):23-39.

Casetti, Emilio. "Optimal Location of Steel Mills Serving the Quebec and Southern Ontario Steel Market." Canadian Geographer 10 (1966):27-39.

Caves, Richard E., and Jones, Ronald W. World Trade and Payments. 2nd ed. Boston: Little, Brown & Co., 1977.

Chacholiades, Miltiades. International Trade Theory and Policy. New York: McGraw-Hill Book Co., 1978.

Chisholm, Michael. Geography and Economics. New York: Praeger, 1966.

Dorfman, Robert; Samuelson, Paul A.; and Solow, Robert M. Linear Programming and Economic Analysis. New York: McGraw-Hill Book Co., 1958.

Eckaus, Richard S. "The Factor Proportions Problem in Underdeveloped Areas." American Economic Review 45 (September, 1955):539-65.

Emerson, David L. Production, Location and the Automotive Agreement. Ottawa: Economic Council of Canada, 1975.

Estle, Edwin F. "A More Conclusive Test of the Heckscher-Ohlin Hypothesis." Journal of Political Economy 75 (1967):886-88.

Ethier, Wilfred. "Some of the Theorems of International Trade with Many Goods and Factors." Journal of International Economics 4 (1974):199-206.

Freeman, Donald B. International Trade, Migration, and Capital Flows. Research Paper No. 146. Chicago: University of Chicago, Department of Geography, 1973.

Friedman, Milton. "The Methodology of Positive Economics." In Essays in Positive Economics. Chicago: University of Chicago Press, 1953.

Hadley, G. Linear Algebra. Reading, Mass.: Addison-Wesley Publishing Co., 1961.

Hall, Robert E. "The Specification of Technology with Several Kinds of Output." Journal of Political Economy 81 (1973):878-92.

Harkness, Jon and Kyle, John F. "Factors Influencing United States Comparative Advantage." Journal of International Economics 5 (1975):153-65.

Harris, Chauncy D. "The Market as a Factor in the Localization of Industry in the United States." Annals of the Association of American Geographers 17 (1954): 92-99.

Harris, Curtis C., and Hopkins, Frank E. Locational Analysis. Lexington, Mass.: Lexington Books, 1972.

Heckscher, Eli. "The Effect of Foreign Trade on the Distribution of Income." In Readings in International Trade. Edited by H. S. Ellis and Lloyd Metzler. Philadelphia: Blakiston, 1949.

Henderson, James M., and Quandt, Richard E. Microeconomic Theory. 2nd ed. New York: McGraw-Hill Book Co., 1971.

Hindley, Brian. The Theory of International Trade. London: Gray-Mills, 1974.

Hoover, Edgar M. The Location of Economic Activity. New York: McGraw-Hill Book Co., 1948.

Intriligator, Michael D. Mathematical Optimization and Economic Theory. Englewood Cliffs, N.J.: Prentice-Hall, Inc., 1971.

Isard, Walter. Location and Space-Economy. Cambridge: MIT Press, 1956.

Johnson, Harry G. The Two-Sector Model of General Equilibrium. Chicago: Aldine, 1971.

Jones, Donald W. "Location and the Demand for Non-Traded Goods: A Generalization of the Theory of Site Rent." Journal of Regional Science, 20 (1980):331-342.

Jones, Ronald W. "Factor Proportions and the Heckscher-Ohlin Theorem." Review of Economic Studies 24 (1956-57):1-10.

_____. "The Structure of Simple General Equilibrium Models." Journal of Political Economy 73 (December, 1965):557-72.

_____. "The Small Country in a Many-Commodity World." Australian Economic Papers 13 (December, 1974): 225-36.

_____. "Twoness" in Trade Theory: Costs and Benefits. Princeton: International Finance Section, Department of Economics, Princeton University, 1977.

Judge, George G., and Takayama, Takashi, eds. Studies in Economic Planning Over Space and Time. Amsterdam: North-Holland Publishing Co., 1973.

Kemp, Murray C. The Pure Theory of International Trade and Investment. Englewood Cliffs, N.J.: Prentice-Hall, Inc., 1969.

_____. Three Topics in the Theory of International Trade. Amsterdam: North-Holland Publishing Co., 1976.

Klaasen, Thomas A. "Regional Comparative Advantage in the United States." Journal of Regional Science 13 (1973):97-105.

Koopmans, Tjalling C. Three Essays on the State of Economic Science. New York: McGraw-Hill Book Co., 1957.

Lande, Paul S. "The Interregional Comparison of Production Functions." Regional Science and Urban Economics 8 (1978): 339-53.

Lefeber, Louis. Allocation in Space. Amsterdam: North-Holland Publishing Co., 1958.

Leontief, Wassily. "Domestic Production and Foreign Trade: The American Capital Position Re-Examined." Economica Internazionale 7 (1954):9-45.

_____. "Factor Proportions and the Structure of American Trade." Review of Economics and Statistics 13 (1956):386-407.

Lindberg, Olof. "An Economic Geographical Study of the Localization of the Swedish Paper Industry." Geografiska Annaler 35 (1953): 28-40.

Lösch, August. The Economics of Location. Translated from 2nd rev. ed. by William H. Woglom and Wolfgang F. Stolper. New Haven: Yale University Press, 1954.

McDivitt, James F., and Manners, Gerald. Minerals and Men. Rev. ed. Baltimore: Johns Hopkins University Press, 1974.

Melvin, James R. "Production and Trade with Two Factors and Three Goods." American Economic Review 58 (December, 1968):1249-68.

Miller, Stephen M. and Jensen, Oscar W. "Location and the Theory of Production: A Review, Summary and Critique of Recent Contributions." Regional Science and Urban Economics 8 (1978): 117-28.

Mills, Edwin S. Studies in the Structure of the Urban Economy. Baltimore: Johns Hopkins Press, 1972.

Mood, Alexander M.; Graybill, Franklin A.; and Boes, Duane C. Introduction to the Theory of Statistics. 3rd ed. New York: McGraw-Hill, 1974.

Moroney, John R. The Structure of Production in American Manufacturing. Chapel Hill: University of North Carolina Press, 1972.

_____. "Natural Resource Endowments and Comparative Labor Costs: A Hybrid Model of Comparative Advantage." Journal of Regional Science 15 (1975):139-50.

Moroney, John R., and Walker, James M. "A Regional Test of the Heckscher-Ohlin Hypothesis." Journal of Political Economy 74 (1966):573-86.

Moses, Leon. "Location and the Theory of Production." Quarterly Journal of Economics 72 (1958):259-72.

Norcliffe, G. B., and Stevens, J. H. "The Heckscher-Ohlin Hypothesis and Structural Divergence in Quebec and Ontario, 1961-1969." Canadian Geographer 23 (1979):239-54.

Ohlin, Bertil. Interregional and International Trade. Rev. ed. Cambridge: Harvard University Press, 1967.

Olds, E. G. "Distributions of Sums of Squares of Rank Differences for Small Numbers of Individuals." Annals of Mathematical Statistics 9 (1938):133-48.

Ponsard, Claude. Économie et èspace. Paris: École Practique des Hautes Études, 1955.

Rawstron, E. M. "Three Principles of Industrial Location." Transactions, Institute of British Geographers 25 (1958): 135-42.

Ricardo, David. The Principles of Political Economy and Taxation. London: J. Murray, 1821.

Rybczynski, T. M. "Factor Endowments and Relative Commodity Prices." Economica 22 (November, 1955):336-41.

Samuelson, Paul A. Foundations of Economic Analysis. Cambridge: Harvard University Press, 1947.

_____. "International Factor-Price Equalization Once Again." Economic Journal 59 (June, 1949):181-97.

_____. "Prices of Factors and Goods in General Equilibrium." Review of Economic Studies 21 (1953-54):1-20.

_____. "The Transfer Problem and Transport Costs." In Readings in International Economics. Edited by Richard E. Caves and Harry G. Johnson. Homewood, Ill.: R. D. Irwin, 1968.

Schwind, Paul J. Migration and Regional Development in the United States. Research Paper No. 133. Chicago: Department of Geography, University of Chicago, 1971.

Serck-Hanssen, J. Optimal Patterns of Location. Amsterdam: North-Holland Publishing Co., 1971.

Smith, David M. Industrial Location. New York: John Wiley & Sons, Inc., 1971.

Stevens, Benjamin H. "Linear Programming and Location Rent." Journal of Regional Science 3 (1963):15-26.

Stolper, Wolfgang, and Samuelson, Paul A. "Protection and Real Wages." Review of Economic Studies 9 (1941):58-73.

Takayama, Akira. Mathematical Economics. Hinsdale, Ill.: Dryden Press, 1974.

Thünen, Johann H. von. Von Thünen's Isolated State. Translated by Carla M. Wortenburg. Edited by Peter Hall. Oxford: Pergamon Press, 1966. Originally published as Der Isolierte Staat in Beziehung auf Landwirtschaft und Nationalökonomie. Hamburg, 1926.

Valavanis-Vail, Stephan. "Leontief's Scarce Factor Paradox." Journal of Political Economy 52 (1954):523-28.

Vanek, Jaroslav. "The Natural Resource Content of Foreign Trade, 1870-1955, and the Relative Abundance of Natural Resources in the United States." Review of Economics and Statistics 41 (1959):146-53.

_____. "The Factor Proportions Theory: The N-Factor Case." Kyklos 21 (1968):749-56.

Weber, Alfred. Theory of the Location of Industries. Translated by Carl J. Friedrich. Chicago: University of Chicago Press, 1929.

THE UNIVERSITY OF CHICAGO
DEPARTMENT OF GEOGRAPHY
RESEARCH PAPERS (Lithographed, 6×9 inches)

Available from Department of Geography, The University of Chicago, 5828 S. University Avenue, Chicago, Illinois 60637, U.S.A. Price: $8.00 each; by series subscription, $6.00 each.

LIST OF TITLES IN PRINT

48. BOXER, BARUCH. *Israeli Shipping and Foreign Trade.* 1957. 162 p.

62. GINSBURG, NORTON, editor. *Essays on Geography and Economic Development.* 1960. 173 p.

71. GILBERT, EDMUND WILLIAM *The University Town in England and West Germany.* 1961. 79 p.

72. BOXER, BARUCH. *Ocean Shipping in the Evolution of Hong Kong.* 1961. 108 p.

91. HILL, A. DAVID. *The Changing Landscape of a Mexican Municipio, Villa Las Rosas, Chiapas.* 1964. 121 p.

101. RAY, D. MICHAEL. *Market Potential and Economic Shadow: A Quantitative Analysis of Industrial Location in Southern Ontario.* 1965. 164 p.

102. AHMAD, QAZI. *Indian Cities: Characteristics and Correlates.* 1965. 184 p.

103. BARNUM, H. GARDINER. *Market Centers and Hinterlands in Baden-Württemberg.* 1966. 172 p.

105. SEWELL, W. R. DERRICK, et al. *Human Dimensions of Weather Modification.* 1966. 423 p.

106. SAARINEN, THOMAS FREDERICK. *Perception of the Drought Hazard on the Great Plains.* 1966. 183 p.

107. SOLZMAN, DAVID M. *Waterway Industrial Sites: A Chicago Case Study.* 1967. 138 p.

108. KASPERSON, ROGER E. *The Dodecanese: Diversity and Unity in Island Politics.* 1967. 184 p.

109. LOWENTHAL, DAVID, editor, *Environmental Perception and Behavior.* 1967. 88 p.

110. REED, WALLACE E., *Areal Interaction in India: Commodity Flows of the Bengal-Bihar Industrial Area.* 1967. 209 p.

112. BOURNE, LARRY S. *Private Redevelopment of the Central City, Spatial Processes of Structural Change in the City of Toronto.* 1967. 199 p.

113. BRUSH, JOHN E., and GAUTHIER, HOWARD L., JR., *Service Centers and Consumer Trips: Studies on the Philadelphia Metropolitan Fringe.* 1968. 182 p.

114. CLARKSON, JAMES D., *The Cultural Ecology of a Chinese Village: Cameron Highlands, Malaysia.* 1968. 174 p.

115. BURTON, IAN, KATES, ROBERT W., and SNEAD, RODMAN E. *The Human Ecology of Coastal Flood Hazard in Megalopolis.* 1968. 196 p.

117. WONG, SHUE TUCK, *Perception of Choice and Factors Affecting Industrial Water Supply Decisions in Northeastern Illinois.* 1968. 93 p.

118. JOHNSON, DOUGLAS L.. *The Nature of Nomadism: A Comparative Study of Pastoral Migrations in Southwestern Asia and Northern Africa.* 1969. 200 p.

119. DIENES, LESLIE. *Locational Factors and Locational Developments in the Soviet Chemical Industry.* 1969. 262 p.

120. MIHELIČ, DUŠAN. *The Political Element in the Port Geography of Trieste.* 1969. 104 p.

121. BAUMANN, DUANE D. *The Recreational Use of Domestic Water Supply Reservoirs: Perception and Choice.* 1969. 125 p.

122. LIND, AULIS O. *Coastal Landforms of Cat Island, Bahamas: A Study of Holocene Accretionary Topography and Sea-Level Change.* 1969. 156 p.

123. WHITNEY, JOSEPH B. R. *China: Area, Administration and Nation Building.* 1970. 198 p.

124. EARICKSON, ROBERT. *The Spatial Behavior of Hospital Patients: A Behavioral Approach to Spatial Interaction in Metropolitan Chicago.* 1970. 138 p.

125. DAY, JOHN CHADWICK. *Managing the Lower Rio Grande: An Experience in International River Development.* 1970. 274 p.

126. MacIVER, IAN. *Urban Water Supply Alternatives: Perception and Choice in the Grand Basin Ontario.* 1970. 178 p.

127. GOHEEN, PETER G. *Victorian Toronto, 1850 to 1900: Pattern and Process of Growth.* 1970. 278 p.

128. GOOD, CHARLES M. *Rural Markets and Trade in East Africa.* 1970. 252 p.

129. MEYER, DAVID R. *Spatial Variation of Black Urban Households.* 1970. 127 p.

130. GLADFELTER, BRUCE G. *Meseta and Campiña Landforms in Central Spain: A Geomorphology of the Alto Henares Basin.* 1971. 204 p.

131. NEILS, ELAINE M. *Reservation to City: Indian Migration and Federal Relocation.* 1971. 198 p.

132. MOLINE, NORMAN T. *Mobility and the Small Town, 1900–1930.* 1971. 169 p.

133. SCHWIND, PAUL J. *Migration and Regional Development in the United States.* 1971. 170 p.

134. PYLE, GERALD F. *Heart Disease, Cancer and Stroke in Chicago: A Geographical Analysis w* *Facilities, Plans for 1980.* 1971. 292 p.

135. JOHNSON, JAMES F. *Renovated Waste Water: An Alternative Source of Municipal Water Sup* *in the United States.* 1971. 155 p.

136. BUTZER, KARL W. *Recent History of an Ethiopian Delta: The Omo River and the Level of L* *Rudolf.* 1971. 184 p.

139. MCMANIS, DOUGLAS R. *European Impressions of the New England Coast, 1497–1620.* 1972. 147 p

140. COHEN, YEHOSHUA S. *Diffusion of an Innovation in an Urban System: The Spread of Plann* *Regional Shopping Centers in the United States, 1949–1968,* 1972. 136 p.

141. MITCHELL, NORA. *The Indian Hill-Station: Kodaikanal.* 1972. 199 p.

142. PLATT, RUTHERFORD H. *The Open Space Decision Process: Spatial Allocation of Costs a* *Benefits.* 1972. 189 p.

143. GOLANT, STEPHEN M. *The Residential Location and Spatial Behavior of the Elderly: A Canad* *Example.* 1972 226 p.

144. PANNELL, CLIFTON W. *T'ai-chung, T'ai-wan: Structure and Function.* 1973. 200 p.

145. LANKFORD, PHILIP M. *Regional Incomes in the United States, 1929–1967: Level, Distributi* *Stability, and Growth.* 1972. 137 p.

146. FREEMAN, DONALD B. *International Trade, Migration, and Capital Flows: A Quantitative An* *ysis of Spatial Economic Interaction.* 1973. 201 p.

147. MYERS, SARAH K. *Language Shift Among Migrants to Lima, Peru.* 1973. 203 p.

148. JOHNSON, DOUGLAS L. *Jabal al-Akhdar, Cyrenaica: An Historical Geography of Settlement a* *Livelihood.* 1973. 240 p.

149. YEUNG, YUE-MAN. *National Development Policy and Urban Transformation in Singapore: A Stu* *of Public Housing and the Marketing System.* 1973. 204 p.

150. HALL, FRED L. *Location Criteria for High Schools: Student Transportation and Racial Integ* *tion.* 1973. 156 p.

151. ROSENBERG, TERRY J. *Residence, Employment, and Mobility of Puerto Ricans in New York C* 1974. 230 p.

152. MIKESELL, MARVIN W., editor. *Geographers Abroad: Essays on the Problems and Prospects* *Research in Foreign Areas.* 1973. 296 p.

153. OSBORN, JAMES F. *Area, Development Policy, and the Middle City in Malaysia.* 1974. 291 p.

154. WACHT, WALTER F. *The Domestic Air Transportation Network of the United States.* 1974. 98 p.

155. BERRY, BRIAN J. L., et al. *Land Use, Urban Form and Environmental Quality.* 1974. 440 p.

156. MITCHELL, JAMES K. *Community Response to Coastal Erosion: Individual and Collective Adju* *ments to Hazard on the Atlantic Shore.* 1974. 209 p.

157. COOK, GILLIAN P. *Spatial Dynamics of Business Growth in the Witwatersrand.* 1975. 144 p.

159. PYLE, GERALD F. et al. *The Spatial Dynamics of Crime.* 1974. 221 p.

160. MEYER, JUDITH W. *Diffusion of an American Montessori Education.* 1975. 97 p.

161. SCHMID, JAMES A. *Urban Vegetation: A Review and Chicago Case Study.* 1975. 266 p.

162. LAMB, RICHARD F. *Metropolitan Impacts on Rural America.* 1975. 196 p.

163. FEDOR, THOMAS STANLEY. *Patterns of Urban Growth in the Russian Empire during the Nineteer* *Century.* 1975. 245 p.

164. HARRIS, CHAUNCY D. *Guide to Geographical Bibliographies and Reference Works in Russian or* *the Soviet Union.* 1975. 478 p.

165. JONES, DONALD W. *Migration and Urban Unemployment in Dualistic Economic Developme* 1975. 174 p.

166. BEDNARZ, ROBERT S. *The Effect of Air Pollution on Property Value in Chicago.* 1975. 111 p.

167. HANNEMANN, MANFRED. *The Diffusion of the Reformation in Southwestern Germany, 1518–15.* 1975. 248 p.

168. SUBLETT, MICHAEL D. *Farmers on the Road. Interfarm Migration and the Farming of Nonc* *tiguous Lands in Three Midwestern Townships, 1939-1969.* 1975. 228 pp.

169. STETZER, DONALD FOSTER. *Special Districts in Cook County: Toward a Geography of Lo* *Government.* 1975. 189 pp.

170. EARLE, CARVILLE V. *The Evolution of a Tidewater Settlement System: All Hallow's Parish, Mar* *land, 1650–1783.* 1975. 249 pp.

171. SPODEK, HOWARD. *Urban-Rural Integration in Regional Development: A Case Study of Saurashtra, India—1800–1960* . 1976. 156 pp.

172. COHEN, YEHOSHUA S. and BERRY, BRIAN J. L. *Spatial Components of Manufacturing Change.* 1975. 272 pp.

173. HAYES, CHARLES R. *The Dispersed City: The Case of Piedmont, North Carolina.* 1976. 169 pp.

174. CARGO, DOUGLAS B. *Solid Wastes: Factors Influencing Generation Rates.* 1977. 112 pp.

175. GILLARD, QUENTIN. *Incomes and Accessibility. Metropolitan Labor Force Participation, Commuting, and Income Differentials in the United States, 1960–1970.* 1977. 140 pp.

176. MORGAN, DAVID J. *Patterns of Population Distribution: A Residential Preference Model and Its Dynamic.* 1978. 216 pp.

177 STOKES, HOUSTON H.; JONES, DONALD W. and NEUBURGER, HUGH M. *Unemployment and Adjustment in the Labor Market: A Comparison between the Regional and National Responses.* 1975. 135 pp.

179. HARRIS, CHAUNCY D. *Bibliography of Geography. Part I. Introduction to General Aids.* 1976. 288 pp.

180. CARR, CLAUDIA J. *Pastoralism in Crisis. The Dasanetch and their Ethiopian Lands.* 1977. 339 pp.

181. GOODWIN, GARY C. *Cherokees in Transition: A Study of Changing Culture and Environment Prior to 1775.* 1977. 221 pp.

182. KNIGHT, DAVID B. *A Capital for Canada: Conflict and Compromise in the Nineteenth Century.* 1977. 359 pp.

183. HAIGH, MARTIN J. *The Evolution of Slopes on Artificial Landforms: Blaenavon, Gwent.* 1978. 311 pp.

184. FINK, L. DEE. *Listening to the Learner. An Exploratory Study of Personal Meaning in College Geography Courses.* 1977. 200 pp.

185. HELGREN, DAVID M. *Rivers of Diamonds: An Alluvial History of the Lower Vaal Basin.* 1979. 399 pp.

186. BUTZER, KARL W., editor. *Dimensions of Human Geography: Essays on Some Familiar and Neglected Themes.* 1978. 201 pp.

187. MITSUHASHI, SETSUKO. *Japanese Commodity Flows.* 1978. 185 pp.

188. CARIS, SUSAN L. *Community Attitudes toward Pollution.* 1978. 226 pp.

189. REES, PHILIP M. *Residential Patterns in American Cities, 1960.* 1979. 424 pp.

190. KANNE, EDWARD A. *Fresh Food for Nicosia.* 1979. 116 pp.

191. WIXMAN, RONALD. *Language Aspects of Ethnic Patterns and Processes in the North Caucasus.* 1980. 224 pp.

192. KIRCHNER, JOHN A. *Sugar and Seasonal Labor Migration: The Case of Tucumán, Argentina.* 1980. 158 pp.

193. HARRIS, CHAUNCY D. and FELLMANN, JEROME D. *International List of Geographical Serials, Third Edition, 1980.* 1980. 457 p.

194. HARRIS, CHAUNCY D. *Annotated World List of Selected Current Geographical Serials, Fourth, Edition. 1980.* 1980. 165 p.

195. LEUNG, CHI-KEUNG. *China: Railway Patterns and National Goals.* 1980. 235 p.

196. LEUNG, CHI-KEUNG and NORTON S. GINSBURG, eds. *China: Urbanization and National Development.* 1980. 280 p.

197. DAICHES, SOL. *People in Distress: A Geographical Perspective on Psychological Well-being.* 1981. 199 p.

198. JOHNSON, JOSEPH T. *Location and Trade Theory: Industrial Location, Comparative Advantage, and the Geographic Pattern of Production in the United States.* 1981. 107 p.